kalí THEATRE COMPANY

Kali Theatre company in association with
Theatre Royal Stratford East presents:

Calcutta Kosher
Written by Shelley Silas

First performed at Theatre Royal Stratford East
Thursday 10 June 2004.

Theatre Royal Stratford East
Gerry Raffles Square
Stratford
London
E15 1BN

www.stratfordeast.com

kalí THEATRE COMPANY | **Theatre Royal** |
└─ STRATFORD EAST ─┘

Calcutta Kosher
by Shelley Silas

Cast in alphabetical order

Maki	**Seema Bowri**
Silvie	**Shelley King**
Mozelle	**Jamila Massey**
Esther	**Harvey Virdi**

With special guest appearance by **Madhav Sharma** as Siddique

Creative team

Director	**Janet Steel**
Designer	**Magdalen Rubalcava**
Composer	**Sayan Kent**
Lighting Designer	**Flick Ansell**
Assistant Lighting Designer	**Chris Pye**
Assistant Director	**Poonam Brah**
Company Stage Manager	**Nicci Burton**
Graphic Design	**Luke Wakeman**
Set built by	**Hedgehog Construction**

Calcutta Kosher was first produced by Kali Theatre Company in association with Tara Arts at Southwark Playhouse on 4th February 2004, with the following cast:

Maki	Seema Bowri
Silvie	Shelley King
Mozelle	Jamila Massey
Siddique	Richard Santhiri
Esther	Harvey Virdi

THE JEWS OF INDIA

It is probably easier to say what Indian Jews are not, rather than what they are; they are not the Ashkenazi (Eastern European Jews) of most British and American popular culture, they are neither part of the Raj, nor Anglo Indians. They are a culture unique both to India and to international Jewry.

The first records of Jews in India date back to 175BC. Some came to India from Spain during the thirteenth century, others from Portugal and Holland in the sixteenth century. A further group arrived direct from Persia, bypassing Europe altogether. For many, the spice business was a huge attraction, and so they came to India to trade. Three major Jewish communities were established in Calcutta, Bombay and Cochin.

In 1788, at the age of twenty six, Shalom Aaron Hakohen, a descendant of an exile from the Spanish Inquisition, left his birth place of Aleppo, and headed for Basra, then Baghdad, eventually sailing from Bombay to Surat in 1790. He traded in indigo, ivory and coffee among other goods. In 1798 he settled in Calcutta – establishing the first Baghdadi Jewish community in India. He was followed by about 2,000 Sephardi Jews, mostly from Baghdad and Aleppo.

Unlike European Jewry, the Jews in India were never oppressed. At a time when anti-Semitism was on the rise in the rest of the world, India was one of the few countries which was not anti-Semitic, allowing Jews to live freely and follow their own customs without worry of antagonism.

Today, there are as few as thirty Indian Jews living in Calcutta.

Shelley Silas

kalí THEATRE COMPANY

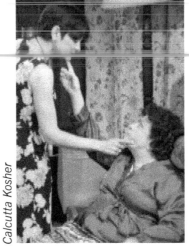

Calcutta Kosher

Sock 'em with Honey

River on Fire

Kali is at the heart of new theatre writing by Asian women, working to promote and present the distinct perspective and experience of Asian women to people from all backgrounds and to celebrate that richness and diversity. We run regular writing workshops, two writer support programmes, *Kali Shorts* and *Kali Futures* and tours of full productions.

Kali is unique in its dedication to working solely with Asian Women writers, allowing the writers the freedom to create the stories and pictures that they want to convey to the audience. At an exciting time when we are increasingly hearing once silent voices telling untold stories in a refreshing and risky way, Kali is working to encourage, support and promote writers from the grass roots level through to experienced playwrights.

Past productions include:

Song for Sanctuary (Rukhsana Ahmad)
Natural World (Joyoti Grech)
The Ecstasy (Anu Kumar)
Black Shalwar (Rukhsana Ahmad)
River on Fire (Rukhsana Ahmad)
Singh Tangos (Bettina Gracias)
Sock 'em With Honey (Bapsi Sidhwa)

kalí THEATRE COMPANY

Kali would to thank Tara Arts, Rasa Restaurants, Cobra Beer, Kuch Kuch, Parmar Foods and Wines, Ben Payne, Dan at Hedgehog, Sue Summers, Samrat Sengupta, Stella Duffy, Jack and Esther Silas, Richard Santhiri, Julia Swift, Mavis Hyman, Melissa Van Tongeren, Julian Torreggiani, Chandana Banerjee, Sara Manasseh, Rivers of Babylon, Jay Visva-Deva, Bhavna Limbachia, Viola Chisholm, Kelly King and all those whose help came too late to be acknowledged here.

Kali Theatre Company Ltd
Colombo Centre
34-68 Colombo Street
London SE1 8DP
020 7021 0000
info@kalitheatre.co.uk
www.kalitheatre.co.uk
Limited Co. No. 258 3595 Registered Charity No. 1071733

Kuch Kuch..

Theatre Royal
STRATFORD EAST

Theatre Royal Stratford East Staff

Artistic

Artistic Director	Philip Hedley
Deputy Artistic Director	Kerry Michael
Resident Director	Dawn Reid
Associate Producer	Robert Miles
New Writing Manager	Ashmeed Sohoye
Writer In Residence	Hope Massiah
Senior Script Associate	Myra Brenner
Theatre Archivist	Murray Melvin
Assistant Archivist	Mary Ling

Musical Theatre Project

Associate Director	ULTZ
Associate Artists	Fred Carl, Clint Dyer, Suzanne Gorman, Robert Lee, Paulette Randall, Deborah Sathe, Zoe Simpson

Administration

Administrative Director	Belinda Kidd
Administrative Manager	Karen Fisher
Development Officer	Zareen Graves
Finance Manager	Paul Canova
Finance Assistant	Elinor Jones

Education

Head of Education	Caroline Barth
Youth and Education Officer	Karlos Coleman, Emma Finlayson

Marketing And Press

Head of Marketing and Sales	Barry Burke
Press	David Bloom, Guy Chapman Associates, Suman Buchar
Marketing Officer	Vincent Fajilagmago
Box Office Manager	Beryl Warner
Box Office Assistants	Asha Bhatti, Saif Osmani, Alice Cook, Davina Campbell, Sharlene Fulgence

Technical

Production Manager	Richard Eustace
Head of Stage	David Williams
Chief Electrician	Stuart Saunders
Deputy Chief Electrician	Dave Karley
Assistant Technician	Helen Atkinson

Front of House

Theatre Manager	Bryan Lewis

| Theatre Royal |
└─ STRATFORD EAST ─┘

Contacting the Theatre

Theatre Royal Stratford East
Gerry Raffles Square
Stratford
London
E15 1BN

Box Office   020 8534 0310
Administration   020 8534 7374
Fax   020 8534 8381
Minicom   020 8279 1114
Press Direct Line   020 8279 1123
Education Direct Line   020 8279 1107

e-mail   theatreroyal@stratfordeast.com
Website_____www.stratfordeast.com

Offices open   Mon – Fri 10am-6pm
Box Office open   Mon – Sat 10am-7pm

Bar open   Mon – Sat 11am-11pm
Food served   Mon – Fri 12am – 2.30pm & 5pm – 7.30pm

Caribbean Flavours in the Theatre Royal Bar

The finest fish and chicken spiced and cooked to perfection by our chef, Wills, as well as a wide range of non-Caribbean food, salads and snacks. Now available in the Theatre Royal Bar.

We would like to thank the Funders and Supporters of Theatre Royal Stratford East: Bridge House Trust, Calouste Gulbenkian Foundation, Financial Service Authority, UBS, Ken Hill Trust, Paul Hamlyn Foundation, The Pidem Fund and Unity Theatre Trust.

Washing Powder supplied by Ecover.

Cast in Alphabetical Order

Seema Bowri Maki

Theatre includes: *Idol Pop*, (Quicksilver Theatre), *The Big Magic, Monkey in the Stars* (Polka Theatre), *Far Pavilions* (West End Demo), *Jungle Book, Dreaming of Home* (Kazzum Arts), *Bollywood Or Bust...Innit!, Don't Look At My Sister...Innit!, Arrange That Marriage...Innit!* (One Nation Under A Grove/Tabularasa Arts). **TV & Film:** *Casualty, Doctors, Coupling* (BBC), *All About Me* (Mondial Productions). **Radio:** *Westway* (BBC World Service), *From Bangladore With Love* (BBC R4) *The Multicoloured Jackal* (Right Angle Productions).

Shelley King Silvie

Theatre includes: *Hobson's Choice* (Young Vic), *Bombay Dreams* (Apollo Victoria), *Besharam* (Soho Theatre/Birmingham Rep), *River on Fire* (Kali), *Ion, The Modern Husband, Orpheus*, (Actors Touring Company), *Women of Troy, Little Clay Cart, Tartuffe* (RNT), *Heer Ranjha, Troilus and Cressida, Danton's Death* (Tara Arts), *The Crutch* (Royal Court), *Damon and Pythias* (Globe), *Death and the Maiden* (Wolsey, Ipswich), Cloud 9 (Manchester Contact), The Innocent Mistress (Derby Playhouse). **TV includes:** *Silent Witness, See How They Run, A Secret Slave* (BBC), two series of *Angels* (BBC), *Tandoori Nights* (Channel 4). **Radio includes:** *The Queen's Retreat, The Tutti Frutti Holy Man, The Eternal Bubble* and *Beyond Purdah*. This is her third production with Janet Steel following *Antigone* (Tara Arts) and *Top Girls* (Royal Northampton).

Jamila Massey Mozelle

Born in Simla and came to England at age 12, later graduating from Kings College London. **Theatre includes:** *The Great Celestial Cow* (Royal Court), *Conduct Unbecoming* (Canada & UK tour), *Song for a Sanctuary* (Kali Theatre/Lyric Hammersmith), *Women of the Dust* (Tamasha/Bristol Old Vic), *The Life & Loves of Mr Patel* (Leicester Haymarket), *Moti Roti Puttli Chunni* (Theatre Royal Stratford East & international tour). **TV includes:** *The Jewel In The Crown*, 33 episodes of *Mind Your Language, All About Me, Doctors, Albion Market, Langley Bottom,*

Churchill's People, Pie In The Sky, Casualty, Arabian Nights, Perfect World, Family Pride, Eastenders. **Film includes:** *Madame Sousatzka,* Chicken Tikka Masala, King of Bollywood, Wild West. Radio: Auntie Satya in *The Archers.* A regular broadcaster for BBC Home and World Services. With her husband, Reginald Massey, she has written books on the music and dance of India.

Madhav Sharma Siddique

Training: RADA. **Theatre includes:** *The King and I* (Tour) *The Accused* (Haymarket) *Last Dance at Dum Dum* (New Ambassadors) *Crazyhorse* (Bristol New Vic/BAC) *Not Just an Asian Babe* (Watermans Theatre) *Indian Ink* (Aldwych Theatre) *High Diplomacy* (Westminster) *Worlds Apart* (Theatre Royal Stratford East) *Blithe Spirit* (Birmingham Rep) *House of the Sun* (Theatre Royal Stratford East) *Twelfth Night* (Theatre Royal Dundee) *Hamlet* (The Howff) *Romeo and Juliet* (Hull Truck NYC/Tour) **TV includes:** *Grease Monkeys, Dr's and Nurses, The Innocents, Dalziel and Pascoe, Holby City, Bugs, Dream Team, Amongst Barbarians, Fighting Back, Shalom Salaam* **Film includes:** *Spivvs, Crust, The Gathering, East is East, Entrapment, Giro City, Wild West, The Awakening, Tangled Web, Shadey, Change of Life, Marriages.* **Audio includes:** radio drama (most recently *A rain of stones)* and talking books (*Kim*). Madhav also directs in the theatre.

Harvey Virdi Esther

Training: Academy Drama School. **Theatre includes:** *The Threepenny Opera,* (Royal National Theatre); *Higra* (West Yorkshire Playhouse); *14 Songs, 2 Weddings and a Funeral, A Tainted Dawn* (Tamasha); *Two Old Ladies, When We Are Married, Romeo & Juliet* (Leicester Haymarket); *Airport 2000* (Rif-Co/Leicester Haymarket); *Twelfth Night* (Tour of Zimbabwe). **TV includes:** *Hear The Silence, Boohbah, The House Across The Street, Baddiel Syndrome, Staying Alive, The Bill, Casualty.* **Film includes:** *Thunderbirds, Bride & Prejudice* (Both due for release summer 2004), *Bend It Like Beckham, Anita & Me, Gran, Guru In Seven.* **Radio includes:** *Singh Tangos, Shakti, Dancing Girls of Lahore, A Yearning, Samsara* (BBC R4).

Creative Team

Shelley Silas Writer

Shelley Silas was born in Calcutta and grew up in north London. Theatre includes: *Calcutta Kosher* (Kali Theatre) at the Southwark Playhouse & UK tour. *Falling,* The Bush Theatre where she was the Pearson writer-in-residence, 2002. *Shrapnel* (Steam Industry) BAC. Plays for Radio 4: devising and co-writing *The Magpie Stories*. *Calcutta Kosher* and *The Sound Of Silence*. She is co-adapting *The Raj Quartet* (with John Harvey), and Hanan al-Shaykh's novel, *Only In London* also for Radio 4 to be broadcast in 2005. Current work includes *Moses Mohammed* for the Bush and *Partitions* for Tamasha Theatre. She has compiled and edited a short story anthology, *Twelve Days* to be published in November 2004 by Virago. Shelley is the writer-in-residence for Clean Break's 2005 production.

Flick Ansell Lighting designer

Also for Kali Theatre Company *River on Fire* and *Sock 'em with Honey*. A selection of Flick's other credits include: Riverside Studios *Majnoun,* Bridewell Theatre *Passion,* BAC *Come Out Eli,* Royal National Theatre *The Good Woman of Setzuan*, Gate Theatre *Mariana Pineda* and *The Increased Difficulty of Concentration*, Chelsea Theatre *Squint* and *Exclude Me,* New End Theatre *Modern Man,* Oval House *La Pucelle* and *Ma Joyce*, Drill Hall *In the Parlour* and *In the Bunker,* Greenwich Theatre *Ali Baba and the Forty Thieves,* Quiconque Theatre Company *Hideaway* and *Big Bad Duvet Terror,* Stratford Circus One *Ruthless,* Royal Academy of Music *Rape of Lucretia* and *Incoronazione di Poppea* and Bush Theatre *In Flame*. As Associate Lighting Designer credits include Royal National Theatre's *Threepenny Opera* and *Star Quality* at The Apollo, Shaftesbury Avenue. Please see www.flickansell.com for full credits and photographs.

Poonam Brah Assistant Director

As a Director, Theatre Includes: *Unfinished Business* (White Bear Theatre, Kennington) *Girl Talk/Sami* (New Experimental Theatre Bombay) *Reader I murdered Him; Black Tigers, Invisible; The I of the Needle* (King's Head Theatre Islington) *Andorra; The Bacchae* (Warwick Arts Centre) As Assistant Director Theatre Includes: *Skellig* (Young Vic) *Hobson's Choice* (Young Vic/Tour) *Sock 'em With Honey* (Kali Theatre/Tour) *Bless The Bride; Billy Liar; Lebenstraum; The Vagina Monologues* (King's Head Theatre Islington) *Song At Twilight (Gielgud Theatre).*

Nicola Burton Company Stage Manager

Training: Rose Bruford Drama College, First Class BA Hons Degree in Stage Management. She has since worked as a Company Stage Manager (on the Book & Re-lights) for the Half Moon Young People's Theatre for their national touring productions of *Gotcha, Cued Up* and *When Snow Falls.*

Nicola has also worked at the Stage Door Manor Performing Arts Centre in New York as a Stage Manager (on the book) for the musicals *Anne of Green Gables* and *Maine*.

Magdalen Rubalcava Designer

Magdalen trained at the National College of Art and Design, Dublin and at the Central School of Art and Design. Theatre includes: *The Little Clay Cart, Tartuffe, Cyrano* (RNT), *September Tide* (Wyndhams), *Heer Ranja* (Globe, Japan), *Cosi fan tutte* and *Don Giovanni* (Pimlico Opera). She was a resident designer at Tara Arts for seven years. Recently she has worked extensively in film including costumes for *The Actors, Angela's Ashes, The Winslow Boy, Moll Flanders, Mary Reilly, Widow's Peak, The Secret Of Roan Inish, The Secret Rapture, The Woman Who Married, Clarke Gable, Troubles, December Bride, The Irish RM, Playboys, Into The West, The Van, The Snapper, The Lion in Winter, Being Julia* and *Asylum*.

Janet Steel Director

Artistic director of Kali Theatre Company. Janet began her career in theatre as an actress, appearing in many theatre, television and radio productions. **Theatre includes:** *Cinders, A Colder Climate* (Royal Court), *Blood Wedding* (Half Moon), *Romeo and Juliet* (Sherman Theatre and Albany Empire), *Oedipus Rex* (Tara Arts). **Television Includes:** *An English Christmas, The Bride, Gems, The Refuge* and *Shalom Salaam*. Janet began her directing Career as an assistant to Tessa Schneideman and The Loose Change Theatre Company. They produced UK premiers by renowned Spanish authors at BAC, which was where Janet directed her first full Length piece, *White Biting Dog* by Judith Thompson. **Directing credits include:** *April in Paris, Bretevski Street, A Hard Rain* and *Top Girls* (The Royal Theatre, Northampton). *Exodus*, as part of the Millennium Mysteries (Belgrade Coventry). Brecht's *Antigone &The Mother, Orpheus Descending, An Ideal Husband, Romeo & Juliet, The Knockey* and *Serious Money* (Rose Bruford College). In 2003 Janet directed Sock 'em with Honey for Kali Theatre, by Bapsi Sidhwa. Janet was recently awarded an MA with Distinction in Theatre Practices, for which she directed From Dawn to Dust by Harprit Sekhon.

CALCUTTA KOSHER

First published in 2004 by Oberon Books Ltd
521 Caledonian Road, London N7 9RH
Tel: +44 (0) 20 7607 3637 / Fax: +44 (0) 20 7607 3629
e-mail: info@oberonbooks.com
www.oberonbooks.com

Reprinted in a new edition in 2004

A catalogue record for this book is available from the British Library.

ISBN: 978-1-84002-454-8

Cover design: Luke Wakeman

Contents

For Mum and Dad – for giving me the best memories and the most delicious food.

Thanks to

Kali Theatre, Tara Arts, Oberon, Stella Duffy, Katie Haines, Fen Watkinson, Helen Cross, Ben Payne, Michael Ezra, Cheryl Isaac, Ian Zach, Shosh and Albert Silas, Trixie Twena, Jack Bradley, Cheryl Robson, Richard Santhiri, Julia Swift, Evie Garratt, Zita Sattar, Chandana Banerjee, Nicola Burton, Sonja Appel and Janet Steel for her tenacity.

And to my grandparents, Molly and Sunny, Lily and Isaac.

Characters

MOZELLE

MAKI

ESTHER

SILVIE

SIDDIQUE

ACT ONE

Scene 1

October. Late afternoon in the ground floor room of a crumbling Calcutta house. A brass ceiling fan remains stationary throughout the play. A couple of pieces of old furniture – including some morahs – are placed around the room. A brand new Apple laptop is open on the table. There are a few cardboard boxes in the room. Doors at the back of the stage lead to a veranda. Just visible outside is the stump of a tree. There is a large black and white photo of the Victoria Memorial on the back wall with a few family photos. As the lights come up, MOZELLE lies back in a wicker day chair, a blanket half covering her. She wears an old dress and several gaudy necklaces and three gold churies (bangles) on her wrist. By her side is SIDDIQUE, her servant. MAKI enters with a glass of water and a bottle of pills, which she gives to SIDDIQUE. MAKI is small and attractive, wears a pair of jeans, T-shirt and chappals. SIDDIQUE gives MOZELLE the pills and exits. MAKI starts to tidy the room.

MOZELLE: Come, come Maki. Stop doing that and come here.

MAKI stops tidying and sits on the bed beside MOZELLE.

MOZELLE takes her hand and strokes it.

MAKI: That tickles.

MOZELLE: You used to like it.

MAKI: I still do, but it tickles.

MOZELLE: What soft skin you have.

MAKI: All the better to stroke.

MOZELLE: Lurki lok kiderhai? (*Where are the girls?*)

19

MAKI: On their way. I must tidy up before they arrive. They'll think we live like pigs. Which of course we don't.

MOZELLE: I don't think I've ever had pig. Have I?

MAKI: I don't know. Have you?

MOZELLE: Of course not. I'm a Jew. Pig is forbidden.

MOZELLE's breathing is laboured.

Soon we'll all be together.

MAKI: You're getting too excited. Calm down. Breath slowly, that's right. Slowly.

Beat.

MOZELLE: What day is it today?

MAKI: Friday.

MOZELLE: Shabbat?

MAKI: Yes.

MOZELLE: Are the candles ready?

MAKI: Of course.

MOZELLE: And the salt?

MAKI: In its little wooden pot.

MOZELLE: You always forget the salt.

MAKI: I do not.

MOZELLE: You do.

Offstage a car horn beeps several times and keeps beeping. Car doors close. A commotion of noise.

MAKI: I'm not ready for them. I need more time. I wanted everything just so.

MAKI runs out onto the veranda, waves.

MOZELLE: Who is it? Who's arrived?

MAKI: Esther, I think.

MOZELLE: Is she wearing boring clothes?

MAKI: Dark blue.

MAKI enters and rushes around clearing up.

MOZELLE: Esther.

MAKI: Shush Ma.

MOZELLE: Silvie would not be seen dead in dark blue.

MAKI: She'll hear you.

MOZELLE: Then let her hear me.

MAKI: She'll think you don't like her.

MOZELLE: Of course I like her.

MAKI: But she'll think you don't. Should I go and help?

MOZELLE: No. Stay here, with me. Siddique will see to her.

There are three knocks at the door.

Come in.

ESTHER enters. She stands by the entrance and looks at MOZELLE. ESTHER wears a simple, dark blue dress, a sensible hat and low-heeled open toe shoes. Everything about her is practical. She stares at her mother, takes in the sight before her.

It's alright. I'm still alive.

MOZELLE opens her arms to ESTHER.

ESTHER walks up to MOZELLE, hugs her.

SIDDIQUE enters with ESTHER's bags, which he puts down. He waits a moment, as if waiting for instructions. When no one speaks to him he exits.

It's good to see you, Esther.

ESTHER: And you.

MOZELLE: It's been a few years since you were here.

ESTHER: A few.

MOZELLE: Ten I think. But who's counting? You know Maki.

ESTHER: Of course.

MAKI: Can I get you anything?

ESTHER: Some water, please.

MAKI: Sure.

ESTHER: Thanks Maki.

MAKI exits.

I'd forgotten how quickly the dust gets into your body.

Beat.

MOZELLE: Don't you have dust in London?

ESTHER is not the most affectionate or tactile woman.

How do I look?

ESTHER: I'm not sure.

MOZELLE: You're not sure? You haven't seen me for two years. How do I look? Do I look the same?

ESTHER: You look pale.

MOZELLE: Do I look sick?

ESTHER: You look sick.

MOZELLE: Then say so. How are my grandchildren and Peter? How is Peter?

ESTHER: Fine, every one is fine. They all send their love.

MOZELLE: And kisses?

ESTHER: What?

MOZELLE: Kisses. Did they send kisses?

ESTHER: Of course.

MOZELLE: Give them to me.

ESTHER: (*Reluctantly.*) This is from Amy. And this is from Alice.

MOZELLE: What about Peter?

ESTHER: Peter sends a kiss too.

MOZELLE offers her cheek to ESTHER.

ESTHER kisses her quickly.

MOZELLE: Just one.

ESTHER kisses her mother again.

That's better. Let me look at you.

MOZELLE examines ESTHER.

You put on weight.

ESTHER: A bit.

MOZELLE: A lot.

ESTHER: A pound or two.

MOZELLE: More than that.

ESTHER: Thanks Molly.

MAKI enters with a tray, a jug and two glasses. She fills a glass and gives it to ESTHER.

MOZELLE: It's been a long time since anyone has called me that. Eh Maki?

ESTHER: I thought you'd be married with a handful of children. Not still living in the black hole?

MAKI: Do you people still call it that?

ESTHER: You people?

MOZELLE: She has a man friend you know. Hidden. Hidden away.

MAKI: Bus! (*Enough.*)

ESTHER: Don't worry, I won't pry. I'll leave that for Silvie.

MOZELLE: If they had degrees in prying, Silvie would be the first to graduate.

MAKI: You look well.

ESTHER: I've become fat, according to my mother.

MOZELLE: But you look well.

ESTHER: Fat and well. (*Beat.*) So what's wrong?

MOZELLE: I had a heart attack.

ESTHER: A heart attack?

MOZELLE: But here I am dear, alive and well. Ready to have some fun with my daughters.

ESTHER: A heart attack? What do you mean a heart attack? (*To MAKI.*) You didn't tell us that. You said she didn't feel well and wanted us to come over.

MOZELLE: I didn't want to worry you.

ESTHER: You think we weren't worried?

MOZELLE: You know how excitable Silvie gets. And flying can be no fun these days, with so much security and pagla (*Mad.*) people who want the world to end.

ESTHER: You should have said. You should have told us Maki.

MOZELLE: Don't blame her. She did as I asked.

ESTHER: What happened?

MAKI: She had a heart attack. She was in hospital for three weeks. She didn't want you to come over until she was home. I called you and then Silvie.

ESTHER: Yes, and we're very grateful to you for calling. But if you'd said a heart attack...

MOZELLE: You would have been here sooner?

ESTHER: Please, don't feel you have to stay any longer, Maki. I'm here now and Silvie will be here soon. I thought I might see her at the airport. The driver suggested we wait, but I didn't want to. It's too hot and too noisy.

MOZELLE: Too chaotic for an English girl?

ESTHER: Calcutta airport isn't my idea of a soothing experience.

MOZELLE: We call it Netaji Subhas Chandra Bose now.

ESTHER: Really?

MAKI: Shall I get on with the Rat Ka Khana (*Dinner.*)?

ESTHER: Dinner?

MOZELLE: There's time.

ESTHER: It's too early for dinner.

MOZELLE: You're all mixed up.

25

ESTHER: I am not mixed up Molly, I am worried and upset and the last thing I can think about right now is food.

MOZELLE: You must always think about food.

MAKI: She wanted her favourites.

MOZELLE: Aloomakalla, Mahmoosa, Chittarnee.

ESTHER: Healthy food for a fat girl?

MOZELLE: Exactly. Do you make our food at home?

ESTHER: Not really. The girls are too fussy.

MOZELLE: Too spoilt.

ESTHER: And Peter likes his food plain.

MOZELLE: Ashkenazie. (*Beat.*) Does he like chicken soup?

ESTHER: Sometimes.

MOZELLE: You should make him Pish Pash.

ESTHER: He calls it baby food.

MOZELLE: I suppose he likes egg and chips? Sunny side up.

ESTHER: Not always.

MOZELLE: Tomato sauce?

ESTHER: Occasionally.

MOZELLE: It is the devil's blood.

ESTHER: It's not that bad.

MOZELLE: Fish balls?

ESTHER: Of course.

MOZELLE: I didn't know fish had them.

MOZELLE laughs to herself.

Maki is helping Siddique with the dinner. She can cook it all you know. Maki, why don't you make some tea?

MAKI: Okay Ma. How do you take it Esther?

MOZELLE: Milk and no sugar.

ESTHER: Milk and one sugar.

MOZELLE: You'll get fatter.

ESTHER: But I'll be sweeter.

MAKI: Ma? Chai?

MOZELLE: Nei nei.

MAKI exits.

ESTHER: What's she calling you ma for?

MOZELLE looks directly at ESTHER.

MOZELLE: She's my child.

ESTHER: Your child?

MOZELLE: Exactly.

ESTHER: What do you mean, your child?

MOZELLE: My love child. I fell in love with a Hindu man.

ESTHER: Of course you did.

MOZELLE: She is our child.

ESTHER: She's your daughter? Is that what you're saying?

MOZELLE: That is exactly what I'm saying.

ESTHER: I know she's been living in this house since she was a child, but she can't be your daughter. It's ridiculous.

MOZELLE: It's true.

ESTHER: And I'm Ghandi.

MOZELLE: Indira or Mahatma?

Beat.

ESTHER: Are you alright?

MOZELLE: Asi dasi. (*So, so.*)

ESTHER: Are you going to be alright?

MOZELLE: Who knows?

ESTHER: Has Dr Chuck prescribed anything?

MOZELLE: There is nothing left to prescribe. I have my pills. If I take any more I'll shake rattle and roll all the way to my grave.

ESTHER: What would you say if I wanted to take you home?

MOZELLE: Home?

ESTHER: Yes.

MOZELLE: To your home?

ESTHER: That's right.

MOZELLE: London?

ESTHER nods.

This is my home. This is where I belong.

ESTHER: There's nothing for you here. Everyone's either moved on...or died.

MOZELLE: Not true. There's still Alfred and Seema. You should have seen Alfred's face when I told him you and Silvie were coming. Lit up like the Victoria Memorial on Independence Day.

ESTHER: It's hardly a community.

MOZELLE: They come here once a week and we play Towli or Carrom. And I win every time. When we are together we look around the room and we remember the old days. You should see us. Three old buddhies. Last year they took me to Gopalpur for a holiday. I sent you a postcard. Did you get it?

ESTHER: No.

MOZELLE: A camel walking across the desert is faster than the post in that damn place. They are such junglies. Behind with the times. Calcutta is the only place to live in India you know.

ESTHER: What about Bombay?

MOZELLE: Too damn noisy.

ESTHER: It isn't exactly quiet in Calcutta.

MOZELLE: This is where I was born and this is where I will die.

ESTHER: You want to die here? All alone?

MOZELLE: I have Maki. Your dadi is buried here. And Ravi's ashes were scattered in the river.

ESTHER: Ravi?

MOZELLE: Maki's dadi. I like to be near them both.

ESTHER: We can make you more comfortable.

MOZELLE: Who is this 'we'?

ESTHER: Me and Peter. The girls would love it. You'll have your own space, anything you need.

MOZELLE: A smelly old woman like me?

ESTHER: You don't smell.

MOZELLE: Usually I do. But Maki hasn't let me eat garlic for weeks so now it's not so bad.

ESTHER: You've been eating garlic?

MOZELLE: Great thick pieces. It keeps away the vampires. And clears my blood. But she said it stinks too much so now I don't eat it.

ESTHER: I really want you to consider coming home with me.

MOZELLE: I will not leave my synagogues. Every Friday night, Faisal arranges prayers at one of them. But you know, I don't think we'll make it tonight. I feel a little tired.

Pause.

ESTHER: I want you to think about it Molly. You're so far away from us.

MOZELLE: You're the one who's far away.

ESTHER: Nothing's changed.

MOZELLE: Maybe not in this house, but Calcutta is more modern than you think. Maki tells me that if you phone to find the time of a train in England, you will speak to someone in Calcutta. Calcutta is where I belong.

ESTHER: But there's nothing here for you now.

MOZELLE: What will I do in London? Watch television, go to the theatre? Eat your English food, with no spices?

ESTHER: We have spices. We can go out for an Indian any time you like. Or Italian, or whatever you want.

MOZELLE: No.

ESTHER: Just listen.

MOZELLE: No.

ESTHER: I've spoken to Peter. We want you to come home. With me.

MOZELLE: And die among strangers?

MAKI enters with tea.

ESTHER: Maki looks well.

MOZELLE: We look after each other.

ESTHER: I thought she'd be living somewhere else by now?

MOZELLE: Maki, my eldest daughter was just saying you should be living somewhere else. Not in this God forsaken place.

MAKI: I like it here.

ESTHER: What's to like? There's nothing to do.

MAKI: It's my home.

MOZELLE: She's a journalist you know.

MAKI: I'm a secretary. For a newspaper. Arts and entertainment pages.

ESTHER: I wouldn't have thought there was much call for that here?

MAKI: Ah well, you should know your birthplace is famous for literature and arts.

ESTHER: Is it?

MAKI: Your room's ready if you need to rest.

ESTHER: I'd really like to have a shower.

MAKI: We only have baths.

ESTHER: Still? Last time we were here Molly said she'd have a shower put in.

MAKI: For you and Silvie. But you never came, so she didn't bother. She likes baths.

ESTHER: A bath will be fine then.

MAKI: I'll run one for you.

MAKI exits.

ESTHER: Why aren't you in hospital. Dr Chuck should know better.

MOZELLE: Dr Chuck does know better. I told him that if he didn't let me go home I would take the hospital out of my will and stop all future donations.

ESTHER: You bribed him?

MOZELLE: Me? Bribe? I hadn't thought of it like that. I suppose I did. How clever of me. (*Pause.*) If you go outside and stand on the tips of your toes, you can just see the synagogue. You must go with Silvie.

ESTHER: Silvie go to synagogue? Pigs will fly.

MOZELLE: They're not kosher you know.

ESTHER: I know.

MOZELLE: Do you eat pig?

ESTHER: No.

MOZELLE: Does Peter?

ESTHER: Of course not.

MOZELLE: I bet Silvie does.

ESTHER: Probably.

ESTHER wipes away sweat from her face. She looks hot and bothered.

MAKI enters.

MAKI: Your bath's running Esther. Siddique will show you where to go.

ESTHER: Thanks.

MOZELLE: Go and wash away the sweat English girl.

ESTHER exits.

MOZELLE leans back.

MAKI remains by her side.

MAKI starts to sing softly.

MAKI: Ni ni baba ni ni, makhan roti, chene. Makhan roti ho kea, chota baba sogea.

MAKI kisses MOZELLE's hand, rests her cheek against MOZELLE.

ESTHER enters, stands quietly at the door.

MAKI sees her, sits up.

ESTHER: (*Whispering.*) Sleeping?

MAKI: Dozing. You don't have to whisper. When she sleeps she sleeps. It's the medication. Nothing wakes her.

MAKI pulls away from MOZELLE and pulls the shawl over her.

ESTHER: Have you got a towel? The girls were helping me pack and I asked them to put one in.

MAKI: I already put a couple in the bathroom for you.

ESTHER: Thanks. I was talking to Molly before and she said…

MAKI: What?

ESTHER: Nothing. Sorry, about earlier. I didn't mean to be rude.

MAKI: You were upset.

33

ESTHER: She was right though, I would have come sooner if I knew it was that serious. Is it serious?

MAKI: I don't know.

Pause.

I took a few days off work.

ESTHER: That's very generous of you.

MAKI: So we could be together. I wanted the house to look nice. It's your home after all.

ESTHER: I don't think it was ever really my home. We were constantly being sent away. To boarding school, and maiden aunts in London. There were always so many people in and out of this place, it was hard to know who was family and who wasn't. It was easy to loose yourself. I could never understand why she didn't leave when my father died. (*Beat.*) What are all these boxes for?

MAKI: She's been clearing.

ESTHER: Throwing away? Not Molly. She's the world's worst horder.

MAKI: No, spiritual clearing. She thinks this place has the unkies.

ESTHER: The evil eye?

MAKI: That's what she thinks.

ESTHER: Has it worked?

MAKI: Who knows?

ESTHER: What do you do all day?

MAKI: Same as you. Work, eat, go out.

ESTHER: It's not your job to cook and clean for my mother.

34

MAKI: Siddique cooks and looks after Ma. Mohammed drives us wherever we want to go. I do whatever I can to help.

ESTHER: Last time we were here she had a helper and you, well, we didn't see much of you.

MAKI: I was on holiday.

ESTHER: With your secret man?

MAKI laughs guardedly.

Just be careful, Silvie will get it out of you when you least expect it. (*Beat.*) You know, I used to envy you. So free and easy, no family ties. You even had your own room.

MAKI: Lucky me.

ESTHER: At least you weren't sleeping on the kitchen floor or outside.

MAKI: Should I have been?

Beat.

ESTHER: I was jealous.

MAKI: Of me?

ESTHER: You were living in my house and you had access to everything I didn't.

MAKI: Low caste girl makes good?

ESTHER: Sorry, no, that's not what I meant. (*Beat.*) They used to take great pride in this house. Every year my father would help paint the outside.

MAKI: I remember.

ESTHER: He'd put on a pair of old trousers and cover his head with a scarf. The whole time he was painting, he felt that he and the servants were the same.

MAKI: He might have thought so, but I doubt very much the servants did.

ESTHER: Every thing gets so dirty from the fumes and smoke from those chulas. I'm not surprised Molly had a heart attack.

MAKI: You remember some Hindustani?

ESTHER: Silvie and me used to speak it fluently when we were small. Now it's just the odd word.

A car horn hoots a few times. And again. Car doors slam. A hubbub of noise.

ESTHER: Maki, I want to take Molly back to London with me. Give her some comfort. I wanted to tell you before Silvie arrived.

MAKI: You want an ally?

SILVIE: (*Off stage in her LA accent.*) Hello, hello.

MOZELLE moves momentarily.

ESTHER: Please don't say anything about this to Silvie.

MAKI: I won't.

Lots of noise, chatter, SILVIE's voice precedes her into the room. She bursts through the doors, Hollywood style. A pifco fan hangs around her neck. SILVIE is one of those women who manage to look perfect even though she has been on a plane for a considerable amount of time.

SIDDIQUE follows close behind with SILVIE's luggage; two large matching designer suitcases and a vanity case. SIDDIQUE has a broad smile on his face.

SILVIE: Lucky, oh Lucky, have you been a bad girl? I came as soon as I could.

SILVIE goes up to MOZELLE and studies MOZELLE, shocked by her appearance.

36

ESTHER: She had a heart attack.

SILVIE: Hello Esther.

ESTHER: She had a heart attack.

SILVIE: A heart attack? You didn't say that when you called? You just said she wasn't feeling too good. If you'd said a heart attack I would have come sooner.

ESTHER: Silvie, this is not Hollywood and Bollywood's on the other side of the country. Keep your voice down.

SILVIE: You been here long?

ESTHER: Not very.

SILVIE: God, this heat is unbearable. At least we have a sea breeze in LA.

MAKI: We have the Hooghly.

SILVIE: Not quite the same thing. Look what Tom bought me at the airport. Isn't he thoughtful?

SILVIE switches on the Pifco fan, holds it over ESTHER, then MAKI and then MOZELLE.

MOZELLE waves her hand in front of her face and drifts back to sleep.

ESTHER: Silvie!

SILVIE: (*To SIDDIQUE.*) That one can go in my room. These stay here.

MAKI: (*To SIDDIQUE.*) Dono suitcase lay jao. (*Take the suitcase.*)

SIDDIQUE picks up one suitcase, leaving the vanity case and other case, and exits.

ESTHER: He's not a servant.

SILVIE: I think you'll find he is.

MOZELLE: Silvie, is that you?

SILVIE rushes over to MOZELLE and holds her tightly.

ESTHER: Careful, she's not a toy.

MOZELLE opens her eyes.

SILVIE: Oh Lucky, I thought we'd lost you.

MOZELLE: And now you found me. How are you?

SILVIE: I'm fine. Just fine. You look tired. Are you getting enough sleep?

MOZELLE: Too much.

SILVIE: Why isn't this place properly air-conditioned?

MAKI: She didn't want it.

SILVIE: Those damn fans.

MOZELLE: Let me look at you Silvie.

SILVIE: All they do is run stale air around in circles. Why don't you switch them on?

MAKI: They're broken.

SILVIE: Does nothing in this place work?

ESTHER: Silvie, shut up. She's not well, she had a heart attack.

SILVIE: Why isn't she in hospital?

ESTHER: She was. For three weeks.

MOZELLE: I want to die in my own home.

SILVIE: Die? What kind of talk is that?

MAKI: She's dying.

SILVIE: She's dying?

MAKI: She says she's dying.

SILVIE: She can't just die when she wants to.

MOZELLE: Stop it girls, please. It's like trying to rest in a room full of nervous pigeons.

SILVIE: Why aren't you still in hospital?

ESTHER: She discharged herself.

SILVIE: Maki?

MAKI: She wanted to come home.

MOZELLE: How are Tom and Jerry?

SILVIE: Tom and Terry are fine. They send their love.

MOZELLE: No kisses?

SILVIE: Sure. Always kisses.

SILVIE plants kisses all over her mother.

Well? What's going on? Someone tell me.

ESTHER: She bribed Dr Chuck. If he didn't agree to send her home, no money.

SILVIE: Jesus Christ, Dr Chuck is a corrupt old bastard.

MAKI: Ma doesn't like swearing.

SILVIE: So who's been looking after her?

MAKI: I have.

SILVIE: Well isn't that lucky for Lucky. You know Mozelle comes from Mazel. It means luck. Did I already tell you that?

MAKI: A few times.

SILVIE: Well, we're here now. You don't have to stay, Maki. I'm sure you've got a life, if any one can have a life here.

MAKI: Esther, what about your bath?

ESTHER: Oh, yeah.

SILVIE: Did you see Siddique? He looks older.

ESTHER: He is older.

SILVIE: Hasn't he got a son?

MAKI: In Patna. Siddique visits him once a year. Ma sends him.

SILVIE: I have terrible memories of Patna. Remember that Lucky?

MOZELLE: What are you talking about now?

SILVIE: Our trip to Patna?

MOZELLE: Oh yes. Tell me, tell me again.

SILVIE: She likes this. We had a three-hour delay at Calcutta airport. The plane was the size of a walk-in wardrobe. We were given flimsy cardboard boxes with stale bread, cheese that looked like it had taken up residence, an over ripe tomato and a piece of dried lettuce.

MOZELLE: Did you eat it?

SILVIE: Of course. (*This is an old joke between SILVIE and MOZELLE.*)

MOZELLE: And did you like it?

SILVIE: It was horrible.

MOZELLE laughs.

MOZELLE: And who did you sit next to?

SILVIE: An incredibly unattractive little man. He couldn't believe that I was born in Calcutta and a Jew. So I gave him a brief history of how our ancestors left Baghdad hundreds of years ago. He said I didn't look like a Jew.

MOZELLE: And what did you say?

SILVIE: Oh, and why is that?

MOZELLE: And what did he say?

SILVIE: Because you have a small nose.

MOZELLE: And what did you say?

SILVIE: You don't look like a man.

MOZELLE: And what did he say?

SILVIE: Oh, and why is that?

MOZELLE: And what did you say?

SILVIE: Because you have a small dunda.

MOZELLE laughs and breathes deeply.

SILVIE: It's good to see you.

ESTHER: If only I believed you.

SILVIE: Go on, make my day. (*Pause.*) Did she really bribe Dr Chuck?

ESTHER: Apparently.

SILVIE: Good for her.

ESTHER: She really isn't very well. She says she's dying.

SILVIE: We're all dying. She had a heart attack. Lots of people have heart attacks and live for years. Nowadays, if you don't have a heart attack you're out of fashion. Ronnie Harris, you remember him? Wanted to have sex with you on a stranger's boat that summer you came over, when your breasts were firm as new pillows and your arse was the size of a peach. He had a heart attack only last month. They ripped him apart, had a good look around. Now he has a pace maker and you'd never know anything was wrong. I was telling the man next to me about it on the way over. He was nice, the man next to me. Sort of fat. Cute, but fat. (*Beat.*) You've put on weight.

ESTHER: I hadn't noticed.

MOZELLE: Silvie? Esther?

ESTHER: We're here Molly. It's alright.

SILVIE stands right over MOZELLE.

Not so close, you'll frighten her.

SILVIE: Always the funny one. You know, if you weren't my sister I'd sign you up. Put you on my books, you'd make a fortune.

SIDDIQUE enters with a small bowl of Mahmoosa, a spoon, a napkin, a bowl of Chukla Buckla which he puts on the table. He places the napkin on MOZELLE and holds the bowl of food while she eats.

ESTHER: I thought we were having dinner later?

MAKI: We are. But she eats little and often. We don't want to overload her.

SILVIE: Shouldn't we be doing that?

MAKI: It's what Siddique does. Ma likes it.

SILVIE: What, is he her personal servant now?

MAKI: He's everything.

SILVIE walks over to SIDDIQUE, takes the bowl out of his hand and feeds MOZELLE.

MOZELLE refuses to eat until SIDDIQUE feeds her.

SILVIE: I bought Lucky some clothes from LA.

ESTHER: Just what she needs. Glitter and gold.

SILVIE: Her stuff is worn out. She needs something to brighten up her days. I don't know about you but when I feel low a bit of retail therapy transforms me.

ESTHER: When do you think she'll need to wear new clothes?

SILVIE: She'll get better, she'll go out.

ESTHER: She's not going out.

SILVIE: We could always bury her in it.

ESTHER: Silvie!

SILVIE: She could wear it tonight?

MAKI: Wear what?

SILVIE: Oh, are you still here? You're like some kind of magician.

MOZELLE: She's a journalist.

MAKI: I'm a secretary.

SILVIE: Secretary?

ESTHER: Arts and entertainment.

SILVIE: I wouldn't have thought there was much entertainment here.

MAKI: That's just what Esther said.

SILVIE: Aren't you married yet?

ESTHER: She has a man.

MOZELLE: Hidden away.

SILVIE: A man? What kind of a man? Tell me more.

MAKI: There's nothing to tell.

SILVIE: Is he gorgeous? I bet he is.

SIDDIQUE finishes feeding MOZELLE, wipes the corners of her mouth with the napkin.

SIDDIQUE: Hum aloo shuroo karega. (*I'll start the potatoes.*)

MAKI: Utcha. (*Okay.*)

SIDDIQUE exits.

SILVIE: I hardly remember any Hindustani these days. Just chalow and utcha and pass me the jaran. You know, Terry says that even now. Pass me the jaran. It always makes me laugh when she says that. It's become part of her vocabulary. I like it. What did he say? Hum aloo…

ESTHER: Something about potatoes.

SILVIE: Yeah, aloo. I know that.

MAKI: He's preparing the potatoes. We're having a dinner party.

SILVIE: Oh good, I love dinner parties. Who's coming?

MAKI: We are.

SILVIE: Any cute men?

MAKI: No.

SILVIE: Oh.

MAKI: Alfred and Seema might join us later.

SILVIE: They still alive?

MAKI: Very much so.

ESTHER: It's a dinner party for Molly.

MAKI: We're having Mahmoosa, Aloomakalla, Chittarnee.

SILVIE: Anything green?

MAKI: Lime pickle?

SILVIE: Salad?

MAKI: I can chop you some lettuce and tomatoes if you like?

SILVIE: Don't want to get scurvy. So it's kind of like the Last Supper. God, I haven't had that food for ages. Tom says it will send us to an early grave. How the hell do you know the art of Indian-Jewish cooking Maki?

MAKI: Siddique taught me.

ESTHER: Siddique?

MAKI: Ma never cooked. But she said it should be preserved and that the tradition should be kept.

SILVIE: So you're keeping it going?

MAKI: I suppose I am.

ESTHER: It's what Molly wants.

SILVIE: And what Lucky wants Lucky gets. Lucky lucky lucky.

MAKI: I should go and help Siddique.

SILVIE: Off you go then.

MAKI exits.

(*Calling.*) Let us know if you need any help.

ESTHER: And I suppose you'll volunteer if she does?

SILVIE: No, but it looks good to offer. What's she calling her 'ma' for?

ESTHER: A term of endearment. I don't know. Molly said she was her love child.

SILVIE: Her love child? Really?

ESTHER: That's what she said. Apparently she had an affair.

SILVIE: How exciting. Do you believe her?

ESTHER: Don't be insane. Women like her didn't have affairs.

SILVIE: Oh? What kind of women did?

SILVIE slips off her shoes. She has a nose around the boxes.

Does she do that a lot?

ESTHER: Apparently. It's the medication.

SILVIE: Someone moving?

ESTHER: House clearing as in exorcising the past.

SILVIE: Spooky.

ESTHER: Sunny would have hated to see her like this.

SILVIE: God knows why they called him Sunny. He was a moody old bastard.

ESTHER: Have you got anything for a headache.

SILVIE: Probably.

She rummages through her vanity case, removes some smelling salts, holds them under ESTHER's nose.

Tom bought them for me. He said they would take away the stale smell. Of the memories, not me. Or maybe he did mean me?

SILVIE removes a variety of things that include bottles of vitamin pills, a shower cap, a bottle of headache pills. She opens the bottle of headache pills and stares, in disbelief. There are no pills, just a small wrap which she removes.

SILVIE: Oh my God. What the hell is this doing in here?

SILVIE offers ESTHER the wrap.

ESTHER: Will it clear my head?

SILVIE: Guaranteed to.

SILVIE carefully opens the wrap.

ESTHER: Salt?

SILVIE dips her finger into the wrap and rubs the powder into her gums.

SILVIE: Waste not want not.

ESTHER: You carried salt all the way over from LA and now you're rubbing it into your gums?

SILVIE: Yeah, I wouldn't want to get cramp. It's cocaine. I carried cocaine all the way over from LA.

ESTHER: Cocaine?

SILVIE: About a quarter of a gram. I didn't know it was still in there. It's good stuff.

SILVIE puts a bit more on her finger, rubs her gums.

ESTHER: Are you mad? There are easier ways of putting yourself in prison. Why did you do it?

SILVIE: Oh, you know, adventure.

ESTHER: It's some of your herbal stuff.

SILVIE: It's herbal alright.

ESTHER: I don't believe you.

SILVIE: Want to try some?

ESTHER: No.

SILVIE: Ever tried it?

ESTHER: Why would I?

SILVIE: Why wouldn't you? Don't you go to parties?

ESTHER: Not your kind of parties. I just don't see the point in being out of your face…

SILVIE: Off my face…

ESTHER: Off your head…

SILVIE: Out of my head… This is probably the most dangerous thing I've ever done without knowing it. Want to try some? Go on. One thin little line.

ESTHER shakes her head.

SILVIE handles the wrap with great care.

SILVIE: Pass me that.

SILVIE notices their mother's hand mirror.

SILVIE empties the contents of the packet onto the mirror.

ESTHER: What are you doing?

SILVIE: Showing the cocaine how good it looks? You've really never taken any drugs in your life?

ESTHER: Never.

SILVIE: Paracetamol? Aspirin? Anti depressentants? Prozac maybe? Weren't you taking Prozac for a while?

ESTHER: It's not the same.

SILVIE: I treat myself occasionally, to a little surprise, a little suggestion of happiness and you think I'm bad?

ESTHER: I didn't say you were bad.

SILVIE: Well you know what? I am bad. And I love every minute of it. When I take this stuff it's because I want to, not because I have to. Get a credit card out of my bag.

ESTHER: A credit card?

SILVIE: Just get it.

ESTHER: Any one in particular?

ESTHER opens SILVIE's bag, removes a credit card, gives it to SILVIE.

SILVIE cuts the cocaine.

SILVIE: You really should try some of this. It might loosen you up, unblock some of that anal retention.

ESTHER: I am not anally retentive.

SILVIE: It'll get rid of your headache.

ESTHER watches in disgust as SILVIE cuts four long lines, all the time teasing ESTHER.

ESTHER: You could have been stopped and put in prison. They might have thought you belonged to some fundamentalist organisation.

SILVIE: So, do you want some?

ESTHER: No.

SILVIE: Just one little snort. One little sniff. Might be your last chance before you get to fifty.

ESTHER: There are plenty of other things I'd like to do before I get to fifty.

SILVIE: Me too.

ESTHER: I thought you'd done it all?

SILVIE: I'd like to learn another language. Maybe Italian. Bongiorno. Mi chiamo Silvie. We have an Italian cleaner. Her eye sight's terrible but she's pretty. You can't have an unattractive cleaner in LA you know. It gives the family a bad name.

ESTHER: Do you do this often?

SILVIE: Only on Fridays and holy days.

SILVIE takes a rupee note out of her purse, rolls it up tight.

I've never done it with a foreign note before. How exciting.

SIDDIQUE enters quietly and watches the women.

49

ESTHER: Do you have to use her mirror?

SILVIE: You want to go first? It won't kill you.

ESTHER looks at cocaine on the mirror.

SILVIE passes the mirror to her.

Wipe some off with your finger and spread it on your gums.

ESTHER: Like Bonjella?

SILVIE: Yes, just like that.

ESTHER holds the mirror, looks at the powder.

ESTHER hesitates, is about to try some when SIDDIQUE appears between the women.

SIDDIQUE: Bath Karega? (*Ready for your bath?*)

ESTHER jerks backwards, spills all the cocaine as SILVIE watches.

SILVIE: Yes, yes, thank you Siddique.

SIDDIQUE: Utcha.

SIDDIQUE jiggles his head and exits.

SILVIE: Don't worry, there's more for later. Now, what was it you wanted?

ESTHER: Headache pills.

SILVIE: Oh yes. Drugs!

SILVIE finds a packet of headache pills and gives them to ESTHER.

God I hate this place. And I don't like baths. Soaking in your own dirty water. I thought she'd have had a shower put in by now.

ESTHER: You know what it's like. Tomorrow and tomorrow and then it never gets done. There's no sense of urgency. That's how it is. That's how it's always been.

A small stone is thrown in through the doors. Then another and another.

SILVIE: What was that?

ESTHER shrugs.

SIDDIQUE: (*Offstage.*) Hey! Ja pala. (*Hey you. Shoo!*)

SILVIE and ESTHER go out to the veranda.

ESTHER: Who was it?

SILVIE: Some kid.

ESTHER: Was he alone?

SILVIE: Looks like it. Siddique would have got him in the old days. (*Beat.*) Remember the gardens?

ESTHER: And the pond?

SILVIE: Weren't there two?

ESTHER: And ducks. I had baby ducklings for pets.

SILVIE: Oh yeah. I sat on one once. Killed it.

ESTHER: There were geese too.

SILVIE: So noisy.

ESTHER: So smelly.

SILVIE: There were lots of us then.

ESTHER: Not so many now.

SILVIE: All gone.

ESTHER: Moved out.

SILVIE: Moved on.

Pause.

They had parties.

ESTHER: And dancing.

SILVIE: She was a good dancer.

ESTHER: The best.

SILVIE: Tom's a great dancer. When she's settled in LA. we'll take her dancing.

ESTHER: What do you mean settled in LA?

SILVIE: Tom's got the decorators in. We're doing up the spare room. Pink and white.

ESTHER: You want to take her back to LA?

SILVIE: Of course.

ESTHER: I want her to come to London.

SILVIE: London?

ESTHER: To stay with us.

SILVIE: Lucky is not going to spend the last days of her life in North London.

ESTHER: You think she'd prefer LA?

SILVIE: At least the people are prettier.

ESTHER: That all depends what you mean by pretty?

MOZELLE stirs.

MOZELLE: What are you two talking about? Where's Maki?

ESTHER: Helping Siddique.

MOZELLE: Ah yes. For our little dinner party. I saved some pickles for you. From dadi's factory. You remember it? I think you should go and visit the new owners, say hello.

SILVIE: New? They're not new. They bought the place years ago.

MOZELLE: They will be very pleased to see you. Your father would be so upset to see it now. How that man has ruined it. We made pickles and we were proud of them.

SILVIE: Proud of pickles.

MOZELLE: Don't make a joke of it. How do you think we could afford to send you to school in England?

SILVIE: Pickles.

MOZELLE: The very best. Lime, mango, brinjal. I can still taste it.

MOZELLE closes her eyes.

SILVIE: Tom won't touch pickles. He hates anything too spicy and hot.

ESTHER: And how is Tom?

SILVIE: Gorgeous.

ESTHER: Working?

SILVIE: Of course. Always working.

ESTHER: Making any money?

SILVIE holds out her hand, shows off a sparkly ring.

See what he gave me last week. It's inscribed.

SILVIE tries to take it off, she can't.

This damn heat. It says, 'to my darling'.

ESTHER: That's all?

SILVIE: Well, there wasn't enough room for anything else.

ESTHER: 'To my darling.'

SILVIE: That's me, his darling.

ESTHER: Inspired.

SILVIE: I want to show Lucky her presents. I bought something for you too. I hope it fits.

ESTHER: Oh, probably not.

SILVIE goes to one of the suitcases. She searches through it until she finds what she wants, wrapped presents.

SILVIE: One for you, one for Lucky and something for your girls. How are they? Alice must be getting ready for her GCSEs?

ESTHER: She is.

SILVIE: And Amy?

ESTHER: Fine. They're both fine.

SILVIE: Terry had sex for the first time. Of course the bastard broke her heart. Are your girls into boys yet?

ESTHER: Alice has a boy she goes to the cinema with and Amy isn't interested, she's too young. I certainly hope they wait a few years before having sex.

SILVIE: Why? As long as they're careful. We had fun, why shouldn't they?

ESTHER: Some of us waited until we were older.

SILVIE: How much older? Come on. We never really talked about personal stuff. You were always too British about it.

ESTHER: If I didn't talk about it then I certainly don't want to talk about it now.

SILVIE: Oh come on. You tell me and I'll tell you. I bet it was that Bombay boy, Nathan. You always had a crush on him. Sometimes I think you married the wrong man. Did you? Did you marry the wrong man, Esther? Do you wish it had been Nathan?

ESTHER: Don't be ridiculous.

SILVIE: Oh come on. Tell me? Tell me when you had sex for the first time.

ESTHER: It's none of your business.

SILVIE: I was fifteen.

ESTHER clearly does not want to hear.

ESTHER: I don't want to know.

SILVIE: Luckily I didn't have my period.

ESTHER: God you're so crude.

SILVIE: I said period. What's so crude about that? What do you want me to say? Full stop? Luckily I didn't have my full stop? He was real gentle. He undid my bra...

ESTHER: Shut up, Silvie.

SILVIE: Boy, is it easy to get you going.

ESTHER starts to cry. She is clearly upset.

What? What did I do? It was a story, okay, a story.

ESTHER: I don't want her to die.

SILVIE: Neither do I.

ESTHER: Tell me she won't die. Tell me.

SILVIE: Mothers don't die. They just go into hiding.

MAKI enters. She sees ESTHER, her face wet with tears, and immediately thinks something has happened to MOZELLE.

55

She runs over to the bed, sees MOZELLE breathing heavily.

ESTHER feels embarrassed. She gets up, exits onto the veranda.

She doesn't do crying in public. So much for having a big sister. Everyone always thought I was the older one because I acted it. (*Beat.*) Some kid threw some stones in. Has it happened before?

MAKI: A few times.

SILVIE: And you've done nothing?

MAKI: What is there to do?

SILVIE: Tell someone.

MAKI: There isn't anyone to tell.

SILVIE: The police?

MAKI: They won't do anything. It's some kid who has decided this is a bad house.

SILVIE: Why?

MAKI: Because Jews live here?

SILVIE: Jews have always lived here.

MAKI: Times change.

SILVIE: So who's the other one?

MAKI: What?

SILVIE: You said Jews live here, who are the others?

Beat.

MAKI: Me.

SILVIE: Really? I didn't know you were Jewish.

ESTHER enters from the veranda.

Esther, did you know Maki was a Jew?

ESTHER: No.

SILVIE: So, your mother was Jewish?

MOZELLE: Maki?

MAKI: It's alright Ma.

MOZELLE: Did you have your bath, Esther?

ESTHER: I'm too tired.

SILVIE: I have to wash before my skin starts growing things you could sell in the market. Where am I sleeping?

MAKI: In Maisie's room. Siddique will help you with your bags. (*Calling.*) Siddique!

SIDDIQUE enters, takes SILVIE's bags and exits.

SILVIE exits with him.

ESTHER: One day, when I was very small, I was sitting under a tree in the garden. Molly was feeding me a banana, and a baboon came and snatched it away. That's her story anyway. The one she's always told me. And I believed her. I'd believe anything she told me.

MAKI: It's changed a lot.

ESTHER: My father used to take pride in his home. Molly used to have the best parties, invite every one. The place would be scrubbed from top to bottom.

MOZELLE: Why don't you go and rest? We'll call you when dinner is ready.

MAKI: Oh, and don't worry about the pigeons.

ESTHER: Pigeons?

MAKI: Yes.

ESTHER: I have pigeons in my room?

MAKI: Only three. There used to be worse things in there.

ESTHER: What could be worse than pigeons?

MAKI: You don't want to know.

MOZELLE: They're good pigeons. They won't shit on you.

ESTHER: That's alright then. Don't let me sleep too long.

ESTHER exits.

MOZELLE: Come and sit beside me.

MAKI: I need to help Siddique with dinner.

MOZELLE: He doesn't need any help. You know, Siddique knows more about our ways than either of those girls could ever know. Esther is more English than the English and Silvie has turned in to an American nightmare.

Beat.

You will do the blessing tonight?

MAKI: Of course.

MOZELLE: You have everything ready?

MAKI: Yes.

MAKI rests her head on MOZELLE's shoulder.

MOZELLE strokes her.

MOZELLE: Sometimes, I would have two Friday night dinners. If Sunny had to return to the office at night, I would go to your father. Your father would be waiting, ready with food and a glass of something sweet.

MAKI: Ma, don't die, please. Don't die.

MOZELLE: Humara butcha boht rota. Nei, Nei butcha. (*My little one is crying a lot. No, no little one.*)

MAKI: Mein kya karoongi. (*I don't have anyone.*)

MOZELLE: You have two sisters.

MAKI: Hum kea kuraga? Koi nai hai hamara waste. (*What will I do? I don't have anyone.*)

MOZELLE: You have two sisters.

MAKI: They won't care about me. Unhe sirif aapke paise se muthlar hai. (*Just about your money.*)

MOZELLE: Hamara paisa jaiga teen hissa. (*My money will be split three ways.*) Three ways. With enough for Siddique. The house is yours.

MAKI: Ma...

MOZELLE: I've made up my mind.

MAKI: They scare me, Ma.

MOZELLE: Who?

MAKI: Esther and Silvie.

MOZELLE: They scare me too. But Silvie's bark is worse than her bite. And Esther...Esther should have married Nathan.

MAKI: Nathan?

MOZELLE: That good looking boy from Bombay. His father exported pickles from the factory. Whenever he came to Calcutta he brought Nathan with him. That boy would be in and out of this house all the time, like he was one of the family. We always thought he would end up with Esther.

SILVIE's scream fills the house.

Such noise. What is going on?

MAKI exits quickly.

SILVIE: (*Off stage.*) Get rid of it.

MAKI runs into the room with her hands cupped. SIDDIQUE follows. She runs out onto the veranda and shakes her hands over the side.

SIDDIQUE: Ki hollo? (*What happened?*)

MAKI: A cockroach.

SILVIE enters.

ESTHER enters.

SILVIE: Horrid thing. It was crawling up my towel. I could have rubbed it into my head. It could have laid eggs in my scalp.

MOZELLE: When you were little you used to stamp on them with your bare feet.

SILVIE: I did not.

ESTHER: You did. I did too.

MOZELLE: You had such round, fat toes Esther.

ESTHER: We were very good at stamping things out.

MOZELLE: And you Silvie, you would stand over the dead thing and pick up the pieces, one by one.

MAKI: I thought you were sleeping Esther?

ESTHER: I was trying to.

MAKI: Do you mind if I start laying the table?

SILVIE: In here?

MAKI: We always have dinner in here.

SILVIE: What happened to the dining room?

MAKI: There is no dining room.

ESTHER: Since when?

60

MAKI: Last year.

SILVIE: Why?

MAKI: We don't need so many rooms.

SILVIE: You should have sold the place then. Got somewhere smaller.

MOZELLE: What's that?

SILVIE picks up her mother's present and hands it to her.

SILVIE: Look what I got you Lucky. All the way from sunny LA.

MOZELLE: What is it?

SILVIE: A dress.

MOZELLE: Cheap stuff.

SILVIE: It is not cheap. It's a designer dress.

MOZELLE: I can have them made here for next to nothing.

SILVIE: You could wear it tonight.

MOZELLE: Pah! Cupra tik nei hai. (*The clothes are no good.*)

SILVIE: Alright. How about a bit of make up?

SILVIE takes make-up from her vanity case, starts applying it to MOZELLE.

MAKI starts re-arranging the table, clearing it and generally getting things ready for dinner.

MAKI: She's not a doll.

SILVIE: Yes she is, aren't you Lucky? Tickle her and she laughs. Touch her here and her arms move like this.

SILVIE continues to attack MOZELLE's face with make-up.

MAKI takes a table-cloth out of a cupboard.

You'll look beautiful, Lucky. Pops loved it when you looked beautiful. He called you his little Munya. Remember when he took us out for dinner to the Grand. You wore blue satin and pops wore a white DJ.

MOZELLE: We had some fun. Until you drank too much.

SILVIE: Me?

MOZELLE: And had to be helped to the car.

SILVIE: Oh yeah.

MOZELLE: Do I look pretty? Do my daughters think I look pretty?

SILVIE: Prettier than the prettiest woman in the world. I could do you next, Maki.

MAKI: I don't need make up.

MOZELLE: My Maki has a perfect face.

SILVIE: My Maki? All of a sudden it's my Maki?

MOZELLE starts to sing.

MAKI continues laying the table.

MOZELLE: Ni ni ba ba ni ni, makhan roti, chene. Makhan roti ho kea, chota baba sogea. (*Sleep sleep baby sleep sleep. Butter bread sugar. Butter bread finished. Small baby slept.*)

MAKI continues to lay the table, taking out two silver candle sticks from a cupboard. She also takes out a silver goblet, a bottle of wine and a prayer book and two Kippahs, from Iraq. She places these on the table.

MOZELLE walks to the table, where she sits.

The youngest daughter will make Kiddush tonight.

SILVIE: Oh, you know I can't read Hebrew.

MAKI removes the prayer book from the cupboard.

ESTHER: That's pops' book.

ESTHER takes the book from MAKI, looks through it.

Pop's handwriting. During the festivals he used to forget what to say, when to say it, when to have eggs for Passover, so he wrote it all in. He used to call it his script.

MOZELLE: Every Friday night we make Kiddush.

SIDDIQUE enters with a covered loaf of white bread. Uncut.

Fresh bread from Nahoums.

SIDDIQUE starts to exit.

Siddique, age rat idero ko ra-ho. *(Siddique, stay tonight.)*

SIDDIQUE stands by the table behind MOZELLE.

I will light the candles. Maki will make the blessing. Cover your heads.

SILVIE: You said the youngest will make the blessing?

MOZELLE: We have bread and wine. The simple things in life. It's good. Tradition. Continuation.

SILVIE: What's Maki doing making Kiddush?

MOZELLE: She's a Jew.

SILVIE: So?

Beat.

MOZELLE: I am her mother.

SILVIE: You?

MOZELLE: Yes.

SILVIE: Mother as in mother, as in like a mother?

63

MOZELLE: I gave birth to her.

SILVIE: You gave birth to her? Her?

MOZELLE: I told Esther when she arrived, she wouldn't believe me. She thinks I am a mad old woman whose words make no sense.

SILVIE: You gave birth to her? You gave birth to her?

ESTHER: You can't have? It's impossible.

SILVIE: But she's Indian?

MOZELLE: Her father was a Hindu.

SILVIE: This is a joke, right?

MOZELLE: Please, can we say the blessing before the sun sets. Cover your heads.

MAKI takes the old Iraqi Kippah, and places it on MOZELLE's head. MAKI covers her head with the other one.

SILVIE: That's pops'.

MOZELLE: Cover your heads.

SILVIE and ESTHER do nothing.

MAKI: Baruch ata adonai. Elo hey noo melech ha-o-lam. Asher kidshanoo be-mits-vo-tav ve-tsi-va-noo le-had-lik ner shell shabbat. Amen.

MOZELLE lights the candles.

Baruch, ata, adonoi, elohanu, melech haolam, borei, pari ha'goffen. Amen.

MOZELLE: Amen

MAKI gives MOZELLE the goblet of wine, she sips first. ESTHER refuses. SILVIE drinks and MAKI is last.

SILVIE: You're kidding, right?

MOZELLE: Shush.

SILVIE: I mean...

MOZELLE: Be quiet Silvie. Maki, carry on please.

MAKI: Baruch at a, adonai elohanu, melech haolam, ha motzi, lechem, min ha'arezt.

ALL: Amen.

MOZELLE looks for the salt pot.

MOZELLE: Salt?

MAKI goes to the cabinet, takes out a small, wooden pot filled with salt.

MOZELLE tears five small peices of bread.

SILVIE: Three cheers for the Rabbis Lucky and Maki. Hip hip...

MOZELLE dips each piece of bread into the salt, eats the first piece and gives each of the others a piece. ESTHER refuses to take it.

MOZELLE: Shabbat Shalom.

SILVIE: You know, once I looked up Shabbat on my computer spell check. (*Beat.*) It came up as Sherbet. Sherbet Shalom.

MOZELLE eats ESTHER's bread.

ESTHER: I suppose you think that's funny?

SILVIE: Hilarious. Absolutely hilarious. You knew about this?

ESTHER: No.

SILVIE: She told you.

ESTHER: And I told you.

SILVIE: She said women like you didn't have affairs.

65

MAKI: It wasn't an affair.

SILVIE: And you. How can you stand there with my father's things and pretend to be someone you're not?

MAKI: I'm not pretending to be anyone.

SILVIE: How can you?

ESTHER: She called you her love child.

SILVIE: Jesus fucking Christ.

MOZELLE: Silvie, you have a disgusting mouth.

MOZELLE starts to choke.

SILVIE: I have a disgusting mouth? I have a disgusting mouth? What am I supposed to say when my mother announces a new addition to the family? What am I supposed to do? Act like it never happened? Carry on as usual? Perfect timing Lucky, a beautiful sunset and Sabbath prayers. You'll go straight to heaven.

MOZELLE continues to choke.

MAKI: Ma! Ma! Siddique, pani, pani.

SIDDIQUE and SILVIE rush to get water as MOZELLE continues to choke.

MAKI: Ma! Ma!

Chaos then stillness as the lights fade to blackout, except for the flickering of the candles, which remain lit through the play.

End of Act One.

ACT TWO

As before. The candles burn. SILVIE picks at the bread.
MOZELLE dozes in her day chair. MAKI enters.

MAKI: Shall I bring you some food?

SILVIE: No need. (*Beat.*) She seems calmer. Did Dr Chuck
say anything else? You were out there long enough.

MAKI: Just that he'll come again in the morning. She's his
favourite patient you know.

SILVIE: Really? I wonder why? He's a good-looking man,
Maki.

MAKI: He's a married man, Silvie.

SILVIE: Don't let that stop you, Maki. I just said he was
good looking. Anyway, you already have a man.

MAKI: Apparently I do.

SILVIE: You know, Dr Chuck's father delivered me. I
don't suppose he delivered you too?

MAKI: I was born in Darjeeling.

SILVIE: Oh.

SILVIE continues to break and eat pieces of bread.

MOZELLE stirs.

MAKI: You're sure I can't get you something?

SILVIE: If I pick I always feel as though I'm not really
eating. It's the stupidest thing, but I keep doing it. (*Beat.*)
I'd forgotten how quickly it gets dark here.

MAKI: No twilight.

MOZELLE quietly starts to say the Shema.

MOZELLE: Shema Israel – Adoni E-Lo-Hey-Noo – Adonai E-Had. Ba-ruch Shem Ke-Vod Mal-Koo-Tow Le-o-Lam Va-Ed.

SILVIE: I wish she'd let us take her to hospital.

MAKI: She was choking, that's all.

SILVIE: Didn't look like it to me.

MAKI: She eats so fast and doesn't chew her food properly.

SILVIE: Won't she let us put her to bed.

MAKI: No. She doesn't want to miss anything.

SILVIE: She never did. She always liked to know what was going on. (*Beat.*) Didn't you ever want to tell us who you were?

MAKI: It was easier to say nothing.

SILVIE: But didn't you ever feel the need to say something? Anything?

MAKI: Not really.

SILVIE: I couldn't have kept my mouth shut.

MOZELLE's praying becomes louder.

I wish she'd stop doing that.

MAKI: It was what Maisie did the night before she died.

SILVIE: Maisie?

MAKI: As if she was getting ready.

SILVIE: Did she know about you too?

MAKI: I think so.

SILVIE: Please don't tell me everyone knew except Esther and me?

MAKI: Not everyone.

SILVIE: So what, she just kept you here like a companion? What did she tell everyone, that you were an orphan and she felt sorry for you? (*Beat.*) She's driving me crazy.

MAKI: Are you always so hard?

SILVIE: I've been known to be even harder. My therapist calls it survival. Silvie, she says, you must open up and allow yourself to feel, to respond. Helen, I say, I am responding, it just looks like I'm not. Besides, if I responded in the way everyone else did, I'd never stop crying. You know, I could do with something a little more substantial. All this bread isn't doing me any good.

MAKI: I'll go and ask Siddique.

MAKI exits.

SILVIE: Why do you keep doing that?

MOZELLE: I'm dying.

SILVIE: You're not dying.

MOZELLE: I'm dying so I'm praying.

SILVIE: You're not dying. You're just having a bad hair day.

MOZELLE: What were you saying to Maki?

SILVIE: Nothing.

MOZELLE: Won't Esther come down?

SILVIE: She won't look at me let alone talk to me. She's hiding under the sheets. Afraid the pigeons will crap on her.

MOZELLE: It's meant to be good luck you know?

SILVIE: Maybe you should tell that to Esther.

MOZELLE: Give her time, she'll come.

SILVIE: I wanted to dress up for dinner, make a real effort. Put on some new clothes.

MOZELLE: You and your new clothes.

SILVIE: I can't believe you didn't tell us. What did you think we'd do?

MOZELLE: Exactly what you're doing now.

SILVIE: So you thought you'd wait until we were older, wiser and then tell us?

MOZELLE: I didn't plan all of this.

SILVIE: Did you plan her?

Pause.

MOZELLE: Of course not.

SILVIE: Are you sure?

MOZELLE: I'm sure.

SILVIE: Why didn't you get rid of her then?

MOZELLE: Get rid of her?

SILVIE: Yeah, you know, have her whipped out?

MOZELLE: Silvie!

SILVIE: You could have had a back street abortion. Wasn't Calcutta famous for its back street abortions?

MOZELLE: I would never have done that.

SILVIE: I don't know whether I'm more angry because of not being told, or because of what you did.

MOZELLE: Maybe you're angry because of both?

SILVIE: Maybe.

MOZELLE: Then tell me off.

SILVIE: Tell you off?

MOZELLE: Isn't that what you really want to do? Shout at me, tell me what I did was wrong and bad?

SILVIE: I can't.

MOZELLE: Why not?

Pause.

SILVIE: Because I don't think it was. I know I should think it was, but I don't. I just wish you'd told me.

SILVIE breaks a piece of bread and eats it, then pushes the bread away.

MOZELLE: We must eat. Siddique will bring food and we will eat.

SILVIE: I'm not hungry anymore.

MOZELLE: You've just eaten some bread.

SILVIE: I'm not hungry hungry.

MOZELLE: Hungry hungry? What is that? You are either hungry or you are not?

SILVIE: I'm not.

MOZELLE: You will eat.

SILVIE: Can't I finish getting dressed?

MOZELLE: Go and get your sister.

SILVIE: I tried.

MOZELLE: Try harder.

SILVIE: Why?

MOZELLE: Because we must talk. All of us.

SILVIE: She won't come down.

MOZELLE: Go and get her.

ESTHER enters with a glass of water.

SILVIE: It's probably best to let her sulk a bit longer.

ESTHER: Who's sulking?

SILVIE: You.

ESTHER: That man will not let me do anything.

MOZELLE: Siddique?

ESTHER: I can't stand having someone do everything for me all the time.

SILVIE: Oh, I don't know, it sounds rather appealing to me. A nice young boy to follow you around all day would be very welcome. Anyway, don't you do everything for Peter and the girls?

ESTHER: That's different. I don't do anything else.

SILVIE: Neither does Siddique.

MOZELLE: Esther, come and sit beside me.

ESTHER sits at the table.

SILVIE: I'm going to finish getting changed. You should as well.

ESTHER: I don't feel like changing.

SILVIE: Go on. Make an effort. It'll make you feel better.

SILVIE exits.

ESTHER breaks off some bread and eats.

MOZELLE: Siddique will bring the food soon.

ESTHER: I'm not hungry.

MOZELLE: Is that hungry, or hungry hungry?

ESTHER: What?

MOZELLE: Come closer.

ESTHER: I'm fine where I am.

MOZELLE: Look at me.

ESTHER looks at MOZELLE. It is all she can do to stop herself from crying.

I will ask Siddique to move you downstairs. To my room. Away from flying creatures.

ESTHER: I don't care about the pigeons.

Beat.

You lied to us.

MOZELLE: I did not lie.

ESTHER: You just didn't tell us?

MOZELLE: Esther!

ESTHER: Do you love her more than us?

MOZELLE: Of course not.

ESTHER: But she's been here all the time?

MOZELLE: You didn't want to live here. Neither did Silvie. And I wasn't going to make you do something you didn't want to. She's always been here, you've known that.

ESTHER: But we didn't know who she really was.

SIDDIQUE enters with a large covered dish. He places it on the table and exits.

MOZELLE: Please call your sisters to come and eat. (*Beat.*) Don't be angry with me.

ESTHER: You lied to us. You had an affair and you lied to us.

MOZELLE: She is your sister.

ESTHER: She'll never be my sister.

MOZELLE: Your half sister.

ESTHER: She'll never be my sister.

MOZELLE: Would you rather I hadn't told you?

Beat.

ESTHER: I didn't need to know.

MOZELLE: Didn't need to or didn't want to?

SILVIE enters, followed by MAKI who carries a bottle of white wine. SILVIE is dressed up, made up and carries a digital camera.

SILVIE: Smile. (*She takes a picture of herself.*) How do I look?

They ignore her. She checks the picture on the camera VDU.

That good? Maki, take one of me and Esther. For the folks back home. Show some teeth Esther.

ESTHER: I'd rather not.

SILVIE: You're so disagreeable. (*Beat.*) Something smells delicious. It's either the food or me.

MOZELLE: I thought you weren't hungry?

SILVIE: I could manage a little something. Esther, why don't you go put on something different?

ESTHER: I don't feel like it.

SILVIE: Well make an effort for once in your life. Do something daring. Do something different. Surprise us.

ESTHER takes a brush out of her bag and brushes her hair. Applies lipstick using her mother's mirror with traces of cocaine on it.

74

SIDDIQUE enters carrying a bowl of pickles.

MAKI uncorks a bottle of wine and pours SILVIE a small glass.

SILVIE downs it in one. SILVIE holds her glass out to MAKI who fills it.

MOZELLE: Where are my pickles?

MOZELLE inhales as SIDDIQUE holds the bowl of pickles under her nose.

Ah, Chukla Bukla.

MAKI puts some pickles on MOZELLE's plate.

MOZELLE, not content, takes more and starts to eat quickly.

MAKI: Ma, not so fast.

MOZELLE: Pani, pani.

MAKI and ESTHER reach for a glass of water at the same time.

ESTHER releases her hand and lets MAKI give it to MOZELLE.

Too much chilli. Too much chilli. Lovely.

ESTHER walks towards the back doors.

SILVIE: Something wrong?

ESTHER: I'm hot.

SILVIE: Menopause?

ESTHER: Just hot.

SILVIE: Well have a cold bath.

ESTHER: I don't want a cold bath.

SILVIE: Well sit down and eat.

ESTHER: Stand up sit down have a bath, eat. Next thing you'll be telling me how proud you are of what she did.

SILVIE: Well actually…

ESTHER: Don't.

SILVIE: I was just going to say that she followed her heart, that's all.

ESTHER: I still don't understand. How come no one noticed the pregnancy? I mean, she must have looked pregnant?

MAKI: She stayed with Nancy in Darjeeling.

SILVIE: Good old Nancy.

MAKI: It was the summer Ma turned forty.

ESTHER: When I had my eleventh birthday party in London. And neither of them came.

MAKI: She always went to Darjeeling for the summer.

SILVIE: Only this time she stayed longer than usual?

ESTHER: Didn't Pops realise anything? He must have noticed something was going on?

MAKI: He was too busy.

ESTHER: He must have known something. He must have seen her, felt her body. How could he not have known?

MAKI: They had separate rooms.

SILVIE: Didn't they have sex?

ESTHER: Didn't you love him?

SILVIE: If they had sex maybe she's really Pops' kid?

MAKI: She stayed in Darjeeling until a month after I was born. After I was born my father came to collect us and I went to live with him. Ma would visit from time to time.

ESTHER: What happened to him?

MAKI: He died when I was four.

ESTHER: How convenient.

MAKI: Since then, all I have ever known is this house.

ESTHER: And us. You knew us?

MAKI: I had something you would never have. I had Ma all to myself and that was enough for me.

SILVIE: How did she meet him?

MOZELLE: He worked in the factory.

ESTHER: For Pops?

MOZELLE: You are sisters in blood.

SILVIE: And pickle.

ESTHER: Doesn't it bother you that she had an affair?

MAKI: It wasn't an affair. She loved him.

MOZELLE: I loved your father too.

SILVIE: Did you Lucky? Did you really love them both?

ESTHER: What did you plan to do?

MOZELLE: We didn't make any plans.

ESTHER: Were you going to leave pops and live with her father?

MOZELLE: He had a name you know. Ravi.

SILVIE: Ravi.

ESTHER: She lied to our father.

SILVIE: Who art in heaven. Hallowed be his name.

MOZELLE starts saying the Shema under her breath.

77

MOZELLE: Shema Israel – Adoni E-Lo-Hey-Noo – Adonai E-Had. Ba-ruch Shem Ke-Vod Mal-Koo-Tow Le-o-Lam Va-Ed.

ESTHER: Stop doing that.

MOZELLE continues to pray.

MOZELLE: Shema Israel – Adoni E-Lo-Hey-Noo Adonai E-Had. Ba-ruch Shem Ke-Vod Mal-Koo-Tow Le-o-Lam Va-Ed.

ESTHER: Stop it.

MAKI: Ma, calm down. Ma.

MAKI rests her hands on MOZELLE's shoulders until she calms down.

SILVIE pours herself some more wine.

ESTHER: I suppose you think you know her better than we do?

MAKI: I would have known her better than you whether she was my mother or not. I've looked after her, cared for her. I'm the one who's been here for her.

MOZELLE: Indian girls look after their mothers.

SILVIE: She didn't have to.

MOZELLE: You girls put us away in fancy homes with a nurse and food I wouldn't eat if I was starving.

ESTHER: How can you say that? I came here offering to take you home.

MOZELLE: You don't really want me?

ESTHER: Yes, I do.

SILVIE: So do I.

MOZELLE: If you'd wanted me you could have asked me long ago.

ESTHER: You wouldn't have come.

MAKI: How do you know? You never asked her?

MOZELLE: I went to London and Los Angeles for holidays, when it suited you, in your time. But you never came here. Except when I asked. (*Pause.*) It is possible to love more than one person at the same time.

SILVIE: Oh Esther knows.

MOZELLE: It is possible.

SILVIE: Don't you Esther?

ESTHER: Be quiet Silvie.

Beat.

MOZELLE: You know, your father was supposed to marry my sister, Maisie. She was prettier than I was, and older. My parents wanted to get rid of her first. But your father didn't want Maisie. He wanted me. He said I would look good on his arm. And my parents agreed. Poor Maisie remained single until we buried her. She died of a broken heart.

SILVIE: Because of Pops?

MOZELLE: Oh no. She was in love with a Hindu boy. He wanted to marry Maisie. It was frowned upon for a Baghdadi Jew to marry an Asknenazai. Marrying a Hindu boy would have killed them.

ESTHER: What happened?

MOZELLE: He married a Hindu girl and Maisie became a recluse, listening to records and dancing alone in her room. Your room.

SILVIE: Great.

ESTHER: Did she know about Ravi?

79

MOZELLE: Yes. She was the one who arranged for me to stay with Nancy in Darjeeling. I loved your father but I was in love with Ravi.

MOZELLE's eyes fill with tears.

I want to rest.

SILVIE: So what do we do now?

MAKI: Eat?

SILVIE: Why not?

ESTHER: All the time we were feeling sorry for you.

MAKI: You never felt sorry for me.

ESTHER: You were lying. You were lying and living off our land.

MAKI: It's mine too. This is my home. This is my mother.

ESTHER: You never belonged to the servants.

MAKI: I never belonged anywhere.

SILVIE: You stayed here.

ESTHER: You had your own room upstairs.

MAKI: It doesn't mean I belonged. Where did you want me to sleep, on the floor? Outside?

SILVIE: Why didn't you say?

MAKI: Why didn't you ask? You never asked. Who did you think I was? A child from the streets? One of Mother Teresa's girls? (*Beat.*) You never asked.

Pause.

SILVIE: Pour me some more wine will you?

MAKI: Get it yourself. I'm not your slave.

SILVIE: Oh, I thought you were?

SILVIE fills her glass.

ESTHER: Don't you think you've had enough to drink?

SILVIE: What's enough? A toast. To our little sister. Who hid in our mother's womb until she was ripe enough to face the world. Oh my God. Do you know what this means? I'm not the baby any more. I'm not the youngest. I'm the in between. The middle one. Tell us things we don't know? You must have some secrets, Maki? You must know things we didn't know. You must have seen things we didn't see?

MAKI: There's nothing to tell.

SILVIE: Spoil sport. You ever go out? Have a life?

MAKI: Of course.

SILVIE: You had sex with this man of yours?

MAKI: It's none of your business.

SILVIE: Well I think it is my business. Is it a real relationship or a platonic one? You know, all talk and no action.

ESTHER: Can't you talk about anything else?

SILVIE: All these years we were coming here and you knew we had the same blood?

ESTHER: Not all the same.

SILVIE: It must have felt strange, when we came over, you knew that we were your sisters. Didn't it feel strange?

MAKI: I never really thought about it.

SILVIE: Oh come on, you must have. How did it feel Maki?

MAKI: You tell me. How did it feel to have your dishes washed?

81

ESTHER: You didn't wash our dishes.

MAKI: Sometimes I did. How did it feel to have your clothes washed and ironed and smelling sweet? To have your shoes polished and your food cooked? Why should it make any difference that it was your sister who was doing it?

ESTHER: We didn't ask you to do it.

MAKI: You still treat Siddique like he owes you something.

SILVIE: It's his job, it's what he's paid for. You were paid.

MAKI: I was never paid. I was part of her.

SILVIE: So how could you do it? How could you pretend to be one of them?

MAKI: One of them? I am one of them. They loved me because of who I was. Siddique knows everything. He's her best friend.

SILVIE: What do they have to talk about?

MAKI: Why don't you ask him?

SILVIE: Because he doesn't speak English.

MAKI: How do you know?

SILVIE: Because he doesn't.

MAKI: Have you ever tried?

Beat.

ESTHER: What will happen to him when she dies?

MAKI: Ma has made arrangements for him. Financial arrangements.

SILVIE: And what about you?

MAKI: I don't know.

ESTHER: You must know.

SILVIE: She's made a will?

MAKI: Yes.

SILVIE: She's left you something?

MAKI: Yes.

ESTHER: What?

SILVIE: Some Jewellery?

MAKI: No.

ESTHER: The house?

SILVIE: You'll be telling us next it's already in your name.

Beat.

MAKI: I didn't ask her to.

ESTHER: We don't need this place. We have our own homes.

SILVIE: How many secrets do you have Maki?

ESTHER: You could have told us.

MAKI: Does it make any difference? Would you have cared about her any more?

ESTHER: We care.

MAKI: Would you have come over more often? Would you have taken more responsibility?

SILVIE: You were doing such a good job.

ESTHER: We have our lives, our families.

MAKI: So do we.

SILVIE: We couldn't be expected to stay in this pit just because she refused to live anywhere else.

MAKI: This is her life. She knows everyone here.

ESTHER: There's hardly any one left in her community.

MAKI: There are enough. And she has other friends.

ESTHER: And what happens when there are none left? What will you do? Be the sole representative of the Calcutta Jews?

MAKI: We can't abandon the synagogues.

SILVIE: You'll have to sometime.

MAKI: We can't just leave them.

SIDDIQUE enters with a covered dish. He puts it on the table. He pours water into MOZELLE's glass.

SILVIE: Maybe you could ship them to a museum somewhere. What do you think Siddique? I said we could ship the synagogues to a museum.

Beat.

SIDDIQUE: Bad idea.

SILVIE: Really?

SIDDIQUE: Really.

SIDDIQUE exits.

SILVIE: He speaks English. Did you teach him?

MAKI: Of course.

SILVIE: Why doesn't he speak to us then?

MAKI: He only speaks when he's spoken to.

SILVIE: What a guy.

Pause.

So, tell us about this man of yours?

ESTHER: Do you plan to make Molly happy before she dies? Announce an engagement?

SILVIE: Who gets engaged these days?

MAKI: Could I have some wine, Silvie?

SILVIE: Sure, Maki.

SILVIE downs her wine and fills a glass for MAKI.

Have you got anything with a bit more bite? This is too sweet.

MOZELLE stirs.

MOZELLE: He was tall and dark and good looking.

SILVIE: What's that Lucky?

MOZELLE: I used to call him my handsome Calcutta boy. What times we would have together.

ESTHER: I feel sick.

SILVIE: Have some wine.

ESTHER: How can you sit there and drink?

SILVIE: What do you want me to do? Call my mother a whore, an adulterer, a liar and a cheat? Is that what you want me to do? Tell her I'm pissed with her because she was never there for us. We have a little sister. Good luck to Lucky. Let's drink a toast. A toast to the mother of all mothers. Lucky. Here's to your long life. Esther, aren't you going to raise a glass to your mother? Come on. Come on Esther. Talk.

ESTHER: There's nothing to say.

SILVIE: I think there's rather a lot to say.

ESTHER: Well maybe I'm just not interested in hearing it right now.

MAKI: We should talk.

ESTHER: ~~If anyone talks it should be us, not you.~~

MAKI: I'm part of this family too.

ESTHER: As far as I'm concerned you were never part of this family. Nothing's changed.

SILVIE: Hey.

ESTHER: Pops would be so hurt.

SILVIE: Pops wasn't such an angel.

ESTHER: What's that supposed to mean?

SILVIE: Are you being naive on purpose? Didn't you ever hear them whispering about the girls on Caraya Street? You're not going to tell me you didn't know?

ESTHER: I knew.

SILVIE: And you think that's okay, you think that it's fine for Pops to screw around while Lucky stayed at home and minded the babies? Is that what you think?

ESTHER: He didn't have a child with another woman.

SILVIE: That we know of. At least she looked after her child.

ESTHER: I don't know how you do it?

SILVIE: It happened, alright? It happened in someone else's past, not mine.

ESTHER: I can't believe this.

SILVIE: What's to believe? We have a sister, we're three not two.

ESTHER: You make it all so simple.

SILVIE: It is simple. If you can love one person in a life time that's great. But two, two, now that's really something else. Lucky followed her heart. At least give her credit for that.

ESTHER: You're a child.

SILVIE: And you are a very sad woman, Esther. You should have pursued Nathan, you should have taken a chance instead of settling for a safe man and a safe life. You've never done anything as dangerous and as exciting as Lucky has. No wonder they all fell in love with her.

ESTHER: You talk too much.

SILVIE: That's what my therapist says. Silvie, you're loud, you talk too much, you have an opinion and you're very demanding. And I thank God I'm loud, that I have an opinion and that I am demanding. Because it means people hear me and sometimes, not always, but sometimes, I get what I want.

SILVIE piles food onto a plate and eats.

ESTHER turns to walk away.

Where are you going now?

ESTHER: To make a call.

SILVIE: Give Peter my love.

ESTHER exits.

I should learn to make this. We could have a family cookbook. The three sisters Indian Jewish Cook Book. All your family favourites and more. You know Siddique never thaught us how to cook. We had servants to do that.

MAKI: You had me.

Beat.

SILVIE: How old is he?

87

MAKI: He never says and we don't ask.

SILVIE: He should be sitting in front of a TV…

MAKI: He can't afford one.

SILVIE: With his wife…

MAKI: She's dead.

SILVIE: And a drink.

MAKI: It's against his religion.

SILVIE: You used to work with him and now he serves you?

MAKI: Never. I'd never let him serve me. He is my equal.

SILVIE: Does he still sleep in the kitchen?

MAKI: He likes it there. He believes it's his place to serve.

SILVIE: And where is your place?

MAKI: Here.

SILVIE: So how can you be his equal?

MAKI: I respect him for who he is, not what he is.

ESTHER enters.

ESTHER: Still drinking?

SILVIE: Still nagging? Want some?

ESTHER: No.

SILVIE: Maki?

MAKI: Yes please.

SILVIE: Oh good. Lucky? Some wine?

MOZELLE: A little. Esther, have a glass of wine with your mother. It has been a long time since we have celebrated together.

ESTHER: What's to celebrate?

MOZELLE: Our ancestors. The first Baghdadis to come
here. And I will be one of the last to leave. I'm going to
the great pickle factory in the sky. You know why we left
Baghdad all those years ago? To trade. In jute and silk.
We were good at it. We were never oppressed in this
country. Did I ever tell you about a man called Shalom
Hákohen?

SILVIE has heard this so many times before.

SILVIE: Yes.

MOZELLE: He established the first Baghdadi community
in Calcutta.

SILVIE: I know.

MOZELLE: You must never forget him. We are all
different. The Bombay Jews. The Bene Israel Jews. The
Cochin Jews. We have our own ways, our own rituals.
You must preserve them. When I die, there will be no
one else. You must keep our tradition, keep our food,
keep our culture and our identity. Without it we are just
like everyone else.

SILVIE: You know, I think my identity keeps changing.
When we were sent to school in England I wanted to
fit in, but I never did. I looked different, I sounded
different. Then I went to America and it started all over
again.

MOZELLE: Do you go to synagogue?

SILVIE: At festivals.

MOZELLE: Every festival?

SILVIE: Some of them. Occasionally.

ESTHER: I buy Russagoolas and Barfi. Peter loves them.

SILVIE: Peter. How is he? Did you get through?

ESTHER shakes her head.

ESTHER: It was engaged.

MAKI: I don't know what I'll do when she's gone.

SILVIE: Have a life.

MAKI: I have a life.

SILVIE: Move out of this place, travel, go away.

MAKI: I have a life. A good life.

SILVIE: You could have a better one.

MAKI: Like you had?

SILVIE: What?

MAKI: You think it was so easy for me? Being here, living here, watching you both come and go. You think it was easy for them, to send you to school in England?

ESTHER: We didn't ask to be sent.

MAKI: They wanted the best for you. They wanted to be proud of their girls. They wanted to show you off.

SILVIE: And what did they want for you?

MAKI: Me?

SILVIE: Yes. You. What aspirations did they have for you?

MAKI: I don't know.

SILVIE: You'll get married.

MAKI: Married?

SILVIE: Yeah, you know, ring on finger, vows that you'll break.

MAKI: Who will marry me?

SILVIE: You have a man.

MAKI: Who will want me? I have no family. Look at me. What do you see? Who do you see? Tell me? Who do you see?

Pause.

SILVIE: You said you have a man?

MAKI: It doesn't mean he'll marry me.

SILVIE: So he does exist?

MAKI: He exists.

SILVIE: Tell us who he is.

Beat.

MAKI: Faisal.

ESTHER: The man who looks after the synagogues?

SILVIE: A muslim?

ESTHER: Very modern.

MAKI: I've got to know him over the years.

SILVIE: Biblically?

Pause.

MAKI: Yes. Who else do I meet? Faisal knows me. He knows us. I trust him.

ESTHER: Does she have any idea?

Beat.

MAKI: Don't be angry with her.

SILVIE: Well I am.

MAKI: What does your therapist say about that?

SILVIE: My therapist says it's unhealthy to feel anger.
I should delve beneath the anger and try to find out
what's really there.

MAKI: And what is really there?

Beat.

SILVIE: Anger. What happened to that other bottle of
wine? Don't get the wrong idea. I drink like this all the
time.

MAKI: Help yourself.

MOZELLE: Girls?

SILVIE: It's alright Lucky.

MOZELLE: I feel so tired. Don't go.

SILVIE: I'm not going anywhere.

MOZELLE: Can you turn me around, so I can look at the
synagogue?

SILVIE: Sure.

ESTHER: What are you doing?

SILVIE: She wants to look at the synagogue.

ESTHER: You can't see it from here.

SILVIE: It's more about the idea of seeing it. You know,
pointing her towards it. Like Mecca.

*SILVIE moves MOZELLE. MOZELLE says the Shema
under her breath.*

MOZELLE: *Shema Israel – Adoni E-Lo-Hey-Noo – Adonai
E-Had. Ba-ruch Shem Ke-Vod Mal-Koo-Tow Le-o-Lam Va-
Ed.*

ESTHER becomes tearful.

SILVIE: Don't cry for Lucky. She has two men waiting for her in heaven.

ESTHER: I'm not crying for her.

SILVIE: Who are you crying for then Esther?

ESTHER: All my life I've been scared. And because I've been scared I've played it safe because that's what I thought I was supposed to do. I met a nice man. We got married, had two nice children. We have a nice house. We live in a nice neighbourhood. We have nice friends. It's so nice. Every Friday we do Kiddush. Everyday Saturday we do the same things. My life is nice. It's so nice it makes me sick.

SILVIE: What's wrong with nice?

ESTHER: If only Molly had told me, trusted me.

SILVIE: It would have been alright?

ESTHER: She didn't give me a chance.

SILVIE: You feel betrayed?

MAKI: Don't hate her Esther.

ESTHER: I don't hate her.

SILVIE: Was there someone else? Before Peter? Was it Nathan?

Pause.

I always knew he had a soft spot for you. He adored you.

ESTHER: He didn't.

SILVIE: He did. I used to watch him watching you.

ESTHER: He never watched me.

MOZELLE: Yes he did.

SILVIE: Whenever he was in this house, he would follow you around like a love-sick puppy.

MOZELLE: His father traded in opium you know?

SILVIE: I though he exported pickles?

MOZELLE: And opium.

SILVIE: Just think, you could have married a drug baron. (*Beat.*) Why don't you give him a call. Is he still living in Bombay?

MOZELLE: Yes.

SILVIE: Call him, Esther.

ESTHER: I can't.

SILVIE: Call him.

ESTHER: What for?

SILVIE: Old time's sake? Because you still love him? Because you'll never know if you don't?

ESTHER: No.

SILVIE: Then I will.

ESTHER: No.

Beat.

SILVIE: Did you already call him? You didn't call Peter did you? You called Nathan.

ESTHER: It was engaged.

SILVIE: Really? Was the line really engaged? Or did Nathan pick up?

ESTHER: He was on his way out.

SILVIE: Is he going to call back?

ESTHER shrugs.

SILVIE: Don't you want him to?

ESTHER: No. No.

SILVIE: I feel a bit sick. I'm not sure if it's the wine, the shock or the jet lag. Everything keeps whirling around up here. A voice keeps saying you have a little sister, you have a little sister and then another voice says no you don't, no you don't.

ESTHER: I wish she hadn't told us. She could have left a small fund for Maki, we wouldn't have known any better. I need a drink.

SILVIE offers ESTHER the bottle of Kiddush wine.

Something non-alcoholic.

MAKI: Let me get you some water.

ESTHER: I can get it myself.

ESTHER pours water from the jug.

MOZELLE: How Sunny used to love it on the veranda. He loved to know that the synagogue was close. He said it made him feel peaceful.

SILVIE: What will happen to them?

MOZELLE: When there are none of us left?

MAKI: They'll be taken care of.

MOZELLE: Faisal, that damn boy who nags us all the time, he will look after them.

SILVIE: There should be somewhere special for synagogues and places of worship that are no longer in use.

MOZELLE: I have made provisions.

ESTHER: For the Calcutta synagogues?

MOZELLE: They are beautiful and should be preserved.

ESTHER: But there'll be no one left to use them?

MOZELLE: You don't burn down a man's house just because he is dead, do you?

Beat.

You will look after Maki?

SILVIE: I think Maki can look after herself.

MOZELLE: Promise me?

SILVIE: I never make a promise I can't keep.

MOZELLE: She has no other family. You are her sisters in blood.

SILVIE: And pickle.

MOZELLE: Siddique. Siddique.

SIDDIQUE enters.

Ow beito humra samnay. (*Come and sit beside me.*)

SIDDIQUE takes his place beside the chair.

SILVIE: Do you think she's uncomfortable?

ESTHER: Well what do you think?

SILVIE: She probably is.

ESTHER: Sometimes you're incredibly stupid.

SILVIE: You're right. I am incredibly stupid. And I'm glad I'm incredibly stupid because if I was as clever as you I'd be leading a perfect life, I'd be happy and I'd have nothing to complain about because I would know everything. But I don't, so I have to learn. We both came here thinking we would take her home. You to your nice detached house, me to my waterfront home in sunny LA Tom's decorating the spare room. I suppose you've built a granny flat at the end of your garden?

Beat.

ESTHER: We're converting the shed.

SILVIE: Calcutta's not good enough for her, but your garden shed is?

MOZELLE: Get me my dress.

SILVIE: What's that Lucky?

MOZELLE: My dress.

SILVIE: The one I bought you? Do you want to wear it now Lucky?

MOZELLE: Get me my dress.

SILVIE: Which dress does she want?

MAKI: Her wedding dress.

SILVIE: Getting married and we didn't know!

MAKI: She wants to wear her wedding dress when she dies.

SIDDIQUE becomes tearful. This is his moment of personal grief.

MOZELLE has a few words with him. They smile and nod at each other.

MAKI goes to the wardrobe, takes out the dress. It is covered in a grey cloth, which MAKI removes. The dress is 1950s wedding dress, off-white from age. It is complete with veil. MAKI takes out a shoe bag, removes a pair of white shoes, a pair of silk stockings and a blue garter. She places them one at a time on a chair.

ESTHER: What are you doing?

MAKI: It's what she wants.

ESTHER: She doesn't know what she wants.

SILVIE: She's decided she's going to die. She doesn't know she's going to die. No one knows they're going to die. We can't put her in that, she'll look ridiculous.

MAKI: I promised her.

MOZELLE: Maki, my Churies (*Bangles.*).

MAKI: It's okay Ma.

> *MAKI stands beside MOZELLE as she removes the three Churies from her wrist. MOZELLE gives them to MAKI. MAKI gives one to SILVIE and one to ESTHER. MAKI places the third one on her own wrist.*

She wanted us to have one each.

MOZELLE: My dress.

MAKI: She wants to wear her dress.

SILVIE: She's not a doll.

MOZELLE: Make me look pretty. Like I did for Sunny. I want to look pretty for him again. And for Ravi. And I want to dance.

SILVIE: You will dance Lucky, you will. Try and rest, Dr Chuck will come again in the morning.

> *MOZELLE starts saying the Shema.*

MOZELLE: Shema Israel – Adoni E-Lo-Hey-Noo – Adonai E-Had. Ba-ruch Shem Ke-Vod Mal-Koo-Tow Le-o-Lam Va-Ed.

> *The following conversation is layered over MOZELLE's praying.*

> *SIDDIQUE holds MOZELLE's hand.*

ESTHER: Call Dr Chuck.

MAKI: He said he was out tonight.

SILVIE: Call someone.

MAKI: There isn't anyone else to call.

SILVIE: Doesn't he have a mobile, a pager?

MAKI: No.

ESTHER: So what do you do in an emergency?

MOZELLE's praying becomes stronger.

SILVIE: Do something.

ESTHER: What can I do?

MAKI: Ma, Ma, calm down.

Gradually MOZELLE becomes quieter and then silent.

SILVIE: Call Dr Chuck.

MAKI: He's out.

SILVIE: Oh come on.

MAKI: She's alright now.

ESTHER: She's not alright. Give me his number and I'll call.

MAKI: She asked him not to come.

SILVIE: Asked him?

MAKI: She spoke with him yesterday. She gave him money.

SILVIE: She bribed him?

MAKI: Yes.

SILVIE: Son of a bitch. I'll have him struck off.

SIDDIQUE: (*Moaning in a low voice.*) Memsahib marghia. Memsahib marghia. (*Memsahib dead. Memsahib dead.*)

All three women gather round the day chair and talk over each other.

SILVIE: Oh Christ.

MOZELLE moans and opens her eyes.

SIDDIQUE smiles and claps his hands.

MOZELLE: My dress, where's my dress?

SILVIE: Oh Lucky.

MAKI: Ma, oh Ma.

MAKI holds MOZELLE's hand.

SIDDIQUE waits at the foot of the day chair.

MOZELLE talks to MAKI in hushed tones and in the odd words of Hindustani.

MOZELLE: Nei, butcha, nei. Don't cry. I'm sorry if I have caused you pain. I did my best.

MAKI: I love you Ma.

MOZELLE mumbles under her breath.

MOZELLE: Silvie?

SILVIE: Here I am.

MOZELLE: Be good.

SILVIE: Always good.

MOZELLE: Look after Maki.

SILVIE: She's not a child.

MOZELLE: I'll come and haunt you.

SILVIE: Promises promises.

MOZELLE: Please.

SILVIE: Maybe. Okay. Okay. She can come and visit whenever she wants.

MOZELLE: Be nice to Esther.

SILVIE: Nice?

MOZELLE: Give a kiss to Tom and Jerry.

SILVIE: Just one?

SILVIE kisses MOZELLE.

MOZELLE: Where is Esther?

SILVIE gestures to ESTHER.

SILVIE: She wants you.

ESTHER: I can't.

SILVIE: This is for her, not you.

ESTHER: I have nothing to say.

SILVIE: You don't have to say anything.

ESTHER: I can't.

SILVIE: Just for once, be brave.

ESTHER approaches MOZELLE.

MOZELLE: You look pretty. Did you get fatter?

ESTHER: Yes I got fatter.

MOZELLE: I loved them you know? I loved them both.

ESTHER: I know.

MOZELLE: You forgive me?

MOZELLE reaches out for ESTHER's hand. Gradually, ESTHER takes it.

Pause.

MAKI takes the veil and places it on MOZELLE's head.

MOZELLE closes her eyes and lays back.

They start to sing. ESTHER remains silent.

MAKI: Ni ni ba ba ni ni, makhan roti, chene. Makhan roti ho kea, chota baba sogea.

MAKI/SILVIE: Ni ni ba ba ni ni, makhan roti, chene. Makhan roti ho kea, chota baba sogea.

SILVIE/MAKI: Ni ni ba ba ni ni, makhan roti, chene. Makhan roti ho kea,chota baba sogea.

They remain still and silent.

SIDDIQUE sings alone, his voice is quiet, broken, full of pain and sadness.

SIDDIQUE: Ni ni ba ba ni ni, makhan roti, chene. Makhan roti ho kea, chota baba sogea.

Fade to blackout. All that remains lit are the candles.

The End.

The Recipes

Granny Lily's Mahmoosa

(*Serves Four*)

1 large onion – chopped

3 tablespoons sunflower oil

4 large potatoes – diced

3 medium size eggs – beaten

1/2 teaspoon turmeric

Salt and pepper to taste

Fresh ginger (optional)

Fresh garlic (for grandma Molly)

Fresh coriander – chopped (optional)

Oven 350/Gas mark 4–5

Fry the onion in a frying pan until brown. Add the diced potatoes and mix well. Add the spices and salt and pepper. The transfer to ovenproof dish, put the beaten egg on top and mix well into the potato mixture. Put in the oven, uncovered. When the potatoes are cooked, remove from the oven and sprinkle with fresh coriander and serve hot – although it is equally delicious cold!

Aloomakallas

(Aloo is Hindi for potato. Makalla is Arabic for fried. Allow two hours for this recipe. It's worth it!)

(Serves Four)

Sixteen King Edwards potatoes – small to medium sized

Peel and par boil the potatoes. Let them drain and cool. Fill a deep pan with sunflower oil and bring to the boil. Add the potatoes (oil should cover them). Bring to the boil, stirring occasionally, until the potatoes form a golden crust. When the potatoes have an all over golden crust, leave and cook again half an hour prior to serving. If you are serving immediately, continue to cook until the outer layer forms a thick deep golden brown crust. Now, you can either remove the potatoes and lay in kitchen paper to remove excess oil. You can also fill your sink with cold water and put the pan in the water for five minutes, turning the potatoes until the bubbles recede. Remove the pan and lay the potatoes in kitchen paper. The outside should have a thick crust and the inside should be fluffy and soft. Good luck!

Chittarnee

(A sweet-sour chicken curry)

(Serves Four)

8 pieces of chicken breast on the bone or joint a roasting chicken, 4–5 lbs

4 large onions

4 large cloves of garlic

Fresh ginger

Fresh or tinned tomatoes (half a tin will do)

3 tablespoon sunflower oil

Salt and pepper to taste

1 teaspoon turmeric (Haldi)

4 tablespoon tomato puree

1 teaspoon chilli powder

4 teaspoon coriander (Dhunia) powder

3 teaspoon cumin (Zeera) powder

2 teaspoon sugar

1/4 cup of cider vinegar

A cup of boiling water

Liquidise or finely chop the onions, garlic, ginger and fresh or tinned tomatoes. Heat the oil. Add the mixture and cook on a low heat until the onions are sautéed. Add salt and pepper to taste, turmeric and tomato puree, chilli, coriander, cumin and sugar. Thoroughly mix. Add the chicken and coat. Lower the heat and cook with the lid on for half an hour or until most of the juices have been absorbed into the chicken. Add the boiling water, cover and simmer until the chicken is soft (half an hour to three quarters of an hour). Add the vinegar. Mix well. Serve hot with rice; pilaw or boiled.

Chukla Bukla

(A mixture of vegetables pickled in vinegar)

I large cauliflower – broken into florets, washed and dried

1lb French beans – sliced

1lb carrots – cut into half inch rings

2oz green chillies (optional)

2 pints malt vinegar

1 teaspoon salt

1/2 teaspoon turmeric (Haldi)

1tsp ginger – finely chopped

Boil the vinegar, add the salt, turmeric and ginger. Add the vegetables, boil for ten minutes. Allow to cool. Pour into cold jars ensuring that the contents are covered with vinegar.

Store in a warm place and allow at least three weeks to mature. Simply delicious.

For further recipes you can buy Mavis Hyman's book *Indian-Jewish Cooking* or *Awafi, compiled and edited by Millie Gubbay, Mozelle Isaac and Gaby Gubbay-Nemes.*

Printed in the USA
CPSIA information can be obtained
at www.ICGtesting.com
LVHW020853171024
794056LV00002B/517